THE A █████████ OF

*Ribbon*

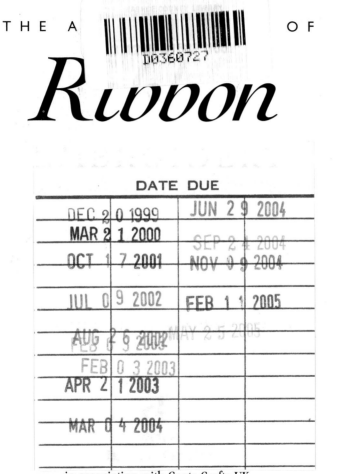

## DATE DUE

| | |
|---|---|
| DEC 2 0 1999 | JUN 2 9 2004 |
| MAR 2 1 2000 | SEP 2 4 2004 |
| OCT 1 7 2001 | NOV 0 9 2004 |
| | |
| JUL 0 9 2002 | FEB 1 1 2005 |
| | |
| AUG 2 6 2002 MAY 2 5 2005 | |
| FEB 2 9 2003 | |
| FEB 0 3 2003 | |
| APR 2 1 2003 | |
| | |
| MAR 0 4 2004 | |
| | |
| | |

in association with Coats Crafts UK

A DAVID & CHARLES BOOK
Published in association with
COATS CRAFTS UK

First published in the UK in 1997

ISBN 0 7153 0634 0

Photography by Alan Duns and David Johnson
Book design by Chris Leishman Design
Printed in Italy by New Interlitho Italia SpA
for David & Charles
Brunel House      Newton Abbot      Devon

# Contents

# Introduction

Embroidering with ribbon is a relaxing and rewarding hobby as it is easy to create the most spectacular effects with just a few, well-placed stitches.

Although it was originally a pastime enjoyed by Victorian ladies, ribbon embroidery is now undergoing a welcome revival as it is well suited to the modern lifestyle. It is quick and easy to do and it employs very few special techniques — most of the stitches are those found in free-style embroidery. It is simply the use of a ribbon, in place of a thread, that creates the stunning effects.

Ribbon embroidery is most commonly used for floral designs as the ribbons brilliantly recreate the natural and free forms of flower petals and leaves. It is possible though, with a little thought, to use simple stitches worked in ribbons to portray any type of image. In fact, the only limitation to ribbon embroidery is your imagination!

Victorian ladies would have worked their ribbon embroideries using ribbons made of silk and this is why this style of embroidery is sometimes referred to as 'silk ribbon embroidery'. Nowadays easy-care polyester ribbons are the popular choice, making the craft much more economical and easily within the reach of every needlewoman.

It is unusual to find an embroidered piece worked entirely with ribbons. Usually the ribbon is there to highlight an area and add extra depth and dimension to the work. Ribbon embroidery can be used in conjunction with almost any other style of embroidery, the two most common choices being cross stitch and free-style embroidery. These styles of embroidery are used to form the basic framework of the design, such as the stems, on which the highlights of ribbon embroidered flowers or leaves will sit. And, as would seem logical, this framework should be completed before the ribbon embroidery is worked.

Ribbon embroidery can be worked on all sorts of fabrics, although the type of fabric is often determined by the other styles of embroidery being used within the piece. Whatever type of fabric is being used, the way in which the ribbon embroidery stitches are worked does not vary.

One of the most endearing qualities of ribbon embroidery is its uniqueness. Although two people may embroider the same design, using the same ribbons and colours, the two finished pieces will look different. This is because every time a stitch is worked using a ribbon the ribbon will twist and fold in a different way, making every single stitch and design element unique.

Ribbon embroidery can be used on all sorts of items – from clothing to household linens or even framed pictures. You will find ideas for using many of the motifs featured in this book on pages 48–49, 78–79 and 122–123, and a range of leaflets are available from Anchor including AEL003, 004, 005 and 006 which feature the embroidery designs shown in the photograph below.

# *Materials*

### Fabrics

A wide variety of different fabrics can be used for ribbon embroidery, including those designed chiefly for counted thread work and surface embroidery. The fabric will need to be firm enough to support the stitching, but its weave must be loose enough to allow the ribbons to pass through without getting damaged. The deciding factor governing the final choice of fabric will be the other styles of embroidery within the design.

If a very lightweight or open weave fabric is to be used, it is advisable to apply a layer of lightweight iron-on interfacing to the back of the fabric before stitching. Not only will this help support the stitching but it will also avoid the chance of any ribbon strands or ends on the back of the work showing through to the right side.

### Embroidery ribbons and threads

The type of ribbon used for embroidery differs from those used as hair ribbons, ties and decorative trims in that it must be very strong, but still needs to be lightweight and also quite narrow. Many embroidery ribbons are available and the most popular choice is a polyester embroidery ribbon — this fits all the necessary criteria and is economically priced. The range of colours available is extensive and the most commonly used widths are 2mm, 4mm and 7mm.

A ribbon embroidery often requires the use of an embroidery thread that exactly matches the colour of the ribbon. On page 128 you will find a colour conversion chart giving the corresponding shade of Anchor Stranded Cotton for every shade of Offray Embroidery Ribbon.

### Needles

The type of needle will be determined by the fabric the embroidery is to be worked on. If it is a freestyle embroidery, a chenille needle is the correct choice as this will easily pierce the fabric. For a design worked on an even weave or Aida fabric, a blunter tapestry needle should be used as the needle should pass between the fabric threads, rather than split them. It may be necessary to use a larger size than would seem appropriate so that the eye of the needle is large enough to thread with the embroidery ribbon.

Any fabric that is suitable for embroidery can have ribbon embroidery worked on it. Even weave fabrics, Aida fabric and firmly woven cottons or linens are all ideal. Packed on neat card bobbins, Offray Embroidery Ribbons are available in a wide variety of colours and there is a matching shade of Anchor Stranded Cotton for every one.

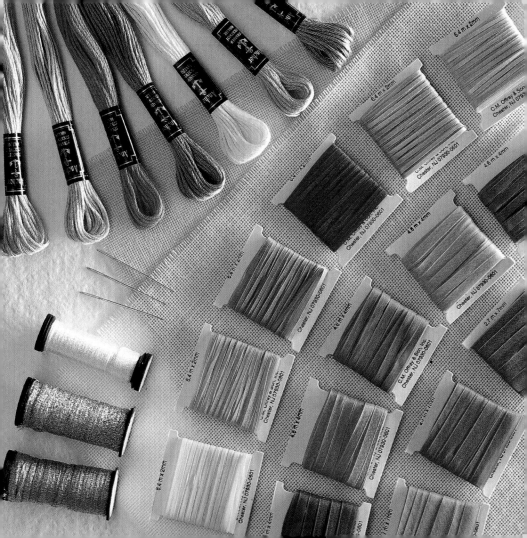

## Working with embroidery ribbon

Embroidery ribbons are far more delicate than many other embroidery threads as their fine weave means they can be easily snagged or creased as they pass through the fabric. To avoid the appearance of the finished work being spoilt by damaged ribbons, always use short lengths of ribbon — about 35–40cm (14–16in) is the recommended length.

### Threading the ribbon on the needle

If the ribbon being used is fairly wide, it will be much easier to thread on to the needle if the end is cut at an angle. This angled end can then easily pass through the eye of the needle.

The part of the ribbon which is folded around the eye of the needle will soon become damaged as the stitches are worked, so it is a good idea to work with this 'fold' very near the free end of the ribbon.

To avoid the ribbon repeatedly unthreading itself, secure it to the needle with a 'stitch'. First thread the needle and slide it along the ribbon for 8–10cm (3–4in). Insert the needle point through the ribbon about 10–15mm (½in) from the cut end (see **Fig 1**) and pull the needle through. This forms a soft 'knot' that secures the needle to the ribbon.

### Securing the ribbon ends

A ribbon embroidery is not usually started by darning the ribbon into the back of the fabric or by tying a knot — the bulk this would create would spoil the finished look. The ribbon ends are secured in other ways instead.

A soft knot can be made in the end of the ribbon, in a similar way to the 'knot' made attaching the needle. Fold over the free end of the ribbon and insert the needle through the double layer of ribbon (see **Fig 2**). Pull the needle through the ribbon carefully, leaving a soft looped knot at the end. Begin the stitching, taking care not to pull the first stitch too tightly as this will cause the soft knot to come undone. Later, this soft knot can be given extra strength by

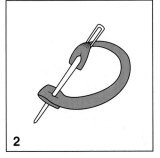

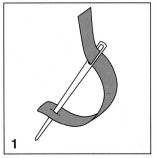

securing it with a few stitches worked in another thread.

A second way to secure the end of the ribbon is by stitching through it. Take the needle and ribbon through to the right side of the fabric for the first time, holding the free end on the wrong side. Position this free end so that when the next stitch is made the needle also passes through this ribbon end (see **Fig 3**), thereby making it secure. Once the embroidery has been completed, the remaining free end can be trimmed away.

## Fastening off

At the end of a line of stitching the best way to secure the ribbon on the wrong side is by making two stitches through an adjacent strand on the back of the work. Take the needle through to the wrong side of the fabric and then make a small stitch through one of the nearby strands of ribbon lying across the work (see **Fig 4**). Take another stitch next to the first and trim away the end of the ribbon.

## Pressing

Ribbon embroidery creates a highly textured surface and to press this in the usual way will destroy the effect. The work can be 'pressed' by stretching it. Begin by pressing any areas that do not feature ribbon work. Take great care not to allow the iron to come too near the areas with ribbons and always press from the wrong side on a soft but firm surface, with a cloth over the fabric. With the right side of the embroidery uppermost, pin the work onto a board (a thick cork tile or a quilter's pressing board is ideal), stretching the fabric so that all creases are removed. Gently mist the work with water and leave to dry before removing the pins.

## Cleaning a ribbon embroidery

To launder a ribbon embroidery, gently wash the item by hand using lukewarm water using a liquid detergent. Rinse it and very carefully squeeze out the excess moisture. Stretch the work over a board as if to 'press' it and leave to dry.

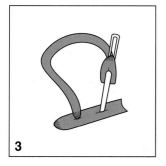

**3**

**4**

## *Ribbon Stitch*

This is one of the few stitches that is exclusive to ribbon embroidery. Based on a simple straight stitch, the effect it creates can be varied quite significantly by altering its length, the tension at which it is worked or the width of embroidery ribbon used.

Start by bringing the needle through the fabric at one end of the line the ribbon stitch is to lie along. Lay the ribbon flat along the line and take the needle back through the fabric at the other end of the stitch, inserting the needle centrally through the embroidery ribbon (see diagram).

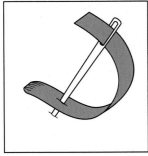

Carefully pull up the embroidery ribbon, keeping it totally smooth and un-twisted, until a tiny fold is formed beyond the point where the needle passed through the ribbon. Take care not to pull the stitch too tight as this will cause the little fold that forms the ribbon stitch to disappear through the fabric, leaving just a simple straight stitch. When working groups of ribbon stitches, ensure that each little fold at the end of the stitches is the same size.

To help keep the section of ribbon that forms the tiny fold completely smooth, try holding another needle against the fabric, to hold the embroidery ribbon flat at the end of the fold. As the embroidery ribbon is pulled up against this second needle, any twists along its length should slip neatly through the fabric, leaving the end of the stitch neat and tidy.

### Daisy Pot

Simple groups of ribbon stitches radiating out from one central point can be used to form flower heads that can resemble any type of flower. Here all the daisies were formed in exactly the same way — only the length of each stitch, the number of stitches worked and, in certain cases, the ribbon width varied.

Worked on Aida fabric, this design used only Ribbon Stitch — even the pot and ferns were worked in this way. The ferns were worked using a narrow 2mm Offray Embroidery Ribbon, colour 584. The pot was formed using 4mm Offray Embroidery Ribbon, colour 846, the stitches worked close together to form a solid satin stitch-like effect, with the folds of the stitches recreating the lip around the top of the pot. Once these sections were complete, the flower heads could be added. These were worked mainly in 4mm wide Offray Embroidery Ribbon, in colours 707, 745 and 824, with some flowers worked in the wider 7mm ribbon, colour 660.

*Daisy Pot* A trace-off pattern for this design is on page 92 .

## *Gathered Stitch*

By cutting a short length of embroidery ribbon and gathering it to form a small ruffled rosette, an endless variety of floral and pompom motifs can be created. Gathered stitch is best worked using a fairly wide ribbon (such as 7mm) and also requires a matching colour of embroidery thread.

Start by cutting a fairly short length of the embroidery ribbon — about 3cm long is ideal. Thread a sharp needle with matching embroidery thread and bring this thread through to the right side of the

fabric at the point where the stitch is to be made.

Now work a zig-zag line of tiny stitches along the length of embroidery ribbon, but not through the fabric, positioning each stitch about 5mm apart (see diagram) and ensuring stitches are worked close to both cut ends of the ribbon. Insert the needle back through the ribbon at the beginning of the zig-zag line of stitching, and then back through the fabric next to the point where it came through originally. Pull up the thread on the wrong side of the fabric and, as the thread is pulled up, the ribbon will gather up to form a tiny ruffled rosette.

To secure the stitch on the right side of the fabric, a tiny Straight Stitch (see page 20) or French Knot (see page 42) can be worked. Depending on the effect to be created, this securing stitch can be worked in the centre, simply to secure the ribbon in place, or to one side of the centre, forming more of a bell shape.

## Hollyhocks

This design was worked in a combination of Gathered Stitches for the flower heads, Ribbon Stitches (see page 10) for the leaves, and French Knots (see page 42) for the unopened buds and flower centres. The least textured areas should always be completed first, in this case the unopened buds. Next, the flower heads were worked and then the leaves, which were tucked over and under the flower heads. The design was completed by working a French knot centre in the middle of each flower head.

Each flower used two widths of embroidery ribbon, with the upper group of flower heads worked in 4mm ribbon, and the lower in 7mm ribbon. The same widths were used in the same way for the leaves. 4mm and 7mm Offray Embroidery Ribbon, in colours 430, 168, 447 and 570, and Anchor Stranded Cotton, in colours 90, 970, 109, 267 and 301, were also used.

*Hollyhocks* A trace-off pattern for this design is on page 93.

## *Lazy Daisy Stitch*

One of the most commonly used free-style embroidery stitches, this stitch also works exceedingly well with embroidery ribbon, producing a similar shape to that achieved with stranded cotton but with much more depth and texture.

A Lazy Daisy Stitch worked with a wide embroidery ribbon makes a fat, highly textured stitch as the ribbon twists as the loop is pulled up. A very fine ribbon is unlikely to twist much and the effect achieved will be more like that created by a thick thread.

Mixing threads and colours will vary the results achieved significantly. Working the loop part of the stitch in green and the tying straight stitch in pink will create a flower bud. Try, also, working the tying stitch with a matching or toning shade of stranded cotton to create yet another effect — you will find that the cotton will hardly show, leaving just a little loop of ribbon.

To make the stitch easier to work, vary the width of the ribbon used according to the stitch length you are making. Very short stitches will not work properly with a wide 7mm embroidery ribbon.

**Fig 1** Bring the ribbon through to the right side of the fabric at the base point of the stitch. Hold the ribbon down firmly against the fabric with your thumb and then take the needle back through the fabric at the point where it originally emerged.

**Fig 2** Bring the needle back up at the end point of the stitch and gently pull up the ribbon until a loop is formed, ensuring the ribbon loop is underneath the needle.

**Fig 3** Finally, secure the stitch by taking the ribbon over the loop you have just made and passing it back through the fabric again on the other side.

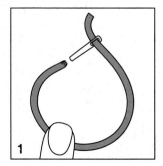

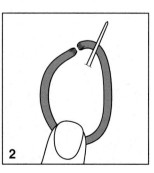

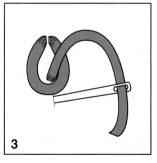

## Floral Swirl

The flowers in this floral motif were formed with five Lazy Daisy Stitches, the larger ones used 4mm Offray Embroidery Ribbon, colour 332, while the tiny flowers used 2mm ribbon, colour 303, to create a more delicate effect. The centre of each flower was made up of French Knots (see page 42) in Anchor Stranded Cotton, colour 301 — one knot for the centre of the smaller flowers, and three for the larger ones.

The large buds were worked as single Lazy Daisy Stitches in 4mm ribbon, with the loop of the stitch in green, colour 530, and the tying stitch in colour 332.

The design was completed with stems of Feather Stitch (see page 60) in Anchor Stranded Cotton, colour 876, topped with a French Knot 'bud' in Anchor Stranded Cotton, colour 2.

*Floral Swirl* A trace-off pattern for this design is on page 93.

## *Ribbon Rose*

One of the easiest roses to make, this consists of a base of embroidery thread with the embroidery ribbon woven around it. Although once complete the embroidery thread will not show, it is advisable to use a matching shade.

When weaving the ribbon over and under the 'spokes', try to leave it quite loose and allow the ribbon to twist and fold as it wants to — this helps to form a natural-looking rose.

Ribbon roses are best worked to fill a circle of 8–12 mm using either a 4 mm or 7 mm ribbon.

**Fig 1** The finished ribbon rose fills a circle. Bring the embroidery thread through the fabric at a point around the outer edge (A). Take the needle back through one fifth of the way around the edge of the circle (B) and bring it back up at the centre point (C), keeping the thread under the needle.

**Fig 2** Take another stitch through the fabric, inserting the needle directly below the centre point at D and bringing it back up midway between D and A (E).

**Fig 3** Take the thread back through the fabric next to the centre point. Make the final stitch by bringing the needle up midway between B and D (F) and taking it back through the centre once more. Fasten off the thread ends very securely as the embroidery ribbon will 'pull' against these threads. At this point, there are five 'spokes' radiating out from the centre of the circle.

**Fig 4** Using the embroidery ribbon, bring the needle up at the centre point, where the 'spokes' meet. Slide the needle under one of the 'spokes'

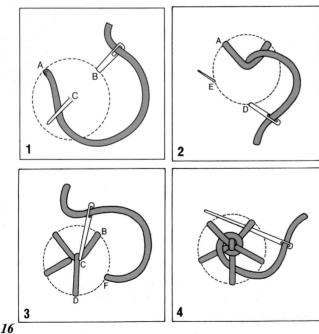

and pull up the ribbon leaving it fairly loose. Working around the 'wheel', miss the next 'spoke' and slide the needle under the following 'spoke', again pulling it up gently. Continue in this way, sliding the needle under every alternate 'spoke' until the circle has been filled and no embroidery thread remains visible. Take the needle back to the wrong side at the end of the next 'spoke' it would pass under and fasten off.

## Ribbon Rose Garland

This garland is made up of groups of ribbon roses, worked in two shades of red Offray Embroidery Ribbon, colours 235 and 260, on a base of Anchor Stranded Cotton, colours 46 and 20. The central rose in each group uses the wider 7 mm ribbon, whilst the smaller ones around this are worked in the 4 mm ribbon. The leaves are worked as Lazy Daisy Stitches using 2mm Offray Embroidery Ribbon, colour 564.

Although every rose of this garland is made in the same way, you can see that no two finished roses will ever look exactly the same.

*Ribbon Rose Garland* A trace-off pattern for this design is on page 94.

17

# *Layered Ribbon Stitches*

Working overlapping rows of Ribbon Stitch will give the surface of the embroidery a heavily textured appearance, with none of the base fabric left visible. This technique is very simple to achieve and can be used to create the effect of feathers, as here, or layers of leaves or grasses.

Ribbon Stitch (see page 10) can either be worked to form wide bands of texture, with the stitches next to each other, or in lines, with one stitch overlapping the end of the previous stitch. Combining these two methods can create

blocks of texture. It is normally the 'flat' end of each Ribbon Stitch (the end where the ribbon first came through the fabric) that will be covered by the folded end of the next stitch.

To work a line of Layered Ribbon Stitch, begin by making the end stitch of the line in the usual way. Work the second stitch so that the needle returns through the fabric very close to the beginning point of the previous stitch so that, when this stitch is completed, the little fold at the end of this second stitch just covers the beginning of the first stitch (see diagram). Continue along the line in this way.

To fill an area with Layered Ribbon Stitch, work further lines of stitching in the same manner, staggering the position of the folded ends of the stitches so that none of the base fabric is left visible.

An area can also be filled by working overlapping bands of Ribbon Stitch. Here each stitch

of each band will be worked next to the previous stitch. A further band is then worked so that the beginning points of the stitches of the previous band are covered.

## Strutting Cockerel

Based on Spanish folk lore designs, the feathers of this cockerel are created by Layered Ribbon Stitches. The body is worked in Long and Short Stitch using Anchor Stranded Cotton, colour 306. The beak is worked in Satin Stitch, the eye is a French Knot and the legs are Stem Stitch, all using stranded cotton, colour 403. Using 2mm Offray Embroidery Ribbon, colour 235, work the head detail and the flower on the body. The neck ruffles are worked using 4mm ribbon in colours 580, 235 and 332. The 7mm ribbon, colours 235 and 332, and 4mm ribbon, colours 580 and 030, are used for the coloured bands of tail feathers. The wing is then worked in 7mm ribbon, colour 660.

*Strutting Cockerel* A trace-off pattern for this design is on page 94.

## Straight Stitch

A simple Straight Stitch worked with an embroidery ribbon will create a totally different effect than if it had been worked with stranded cotton. As even the finest ribbon is much wider than a standard embroidery thread, the ends of the stitch will tend to gather together where the ribbon passes through the fabric. This will add texture to the work and the stitch forms an oval shape on the fabric surface. The fullness of this oval shape will depend on the length of the stitch and the thickness of the ribbon — a short stitch using a wide

ribbon will form a very plump stitch, whilst a long stitch worked in a fine ribbon will appear almost angular.

To work a Straight Stitch with an embroidery ribbon, simply bring the ribbon through to the right side of the fabric at one end of the stitch. Take the needle back through the fabric at the required point and ease the ribbon through gently, ensuring that it is not twisted (see diagram). Should the ribbon twist, carefully pull the ribbon back so that there is a loop on the right side, smooth out the ribbon and then gently pull it through again.

### Flower Patch

Ribbon embroidery is often combined with Cross Stitch embroidery and worked on a Cross Stitch fabric, such as Aida. Here the Flower Patch is outlined in Back Stitch using Anchor Stranded Cotton, colour 970.

The top row of flowers is worked in Ribbon Stitches (see page 10) using 4mm Offray Embroidery Ribbon, colour 430, with a French Knot (see page 42) centre in stranded cotton, colour 289. The stems are Straight Stitch and the leaves are Lazy Daisy Stitch (see page 14) worked using 2mm ribbon, colour 567.

The central band of flowers are Gathered Stitch (see page 12) in 7mm ribbon, colour 332, and the Cross Stitch stems and leaves are worked in stranded cotton, colour 266.

The lower band of Ribbon Roses (see page 16) are worked in 7mm ribbon, colour 168, with stranded cotton, colour 970, as the base stitches. The stems of these roses are Straight Stitch worked using 4mm ribbon, colour 567.

*Flower Patch* A chart for this design is on page 111.

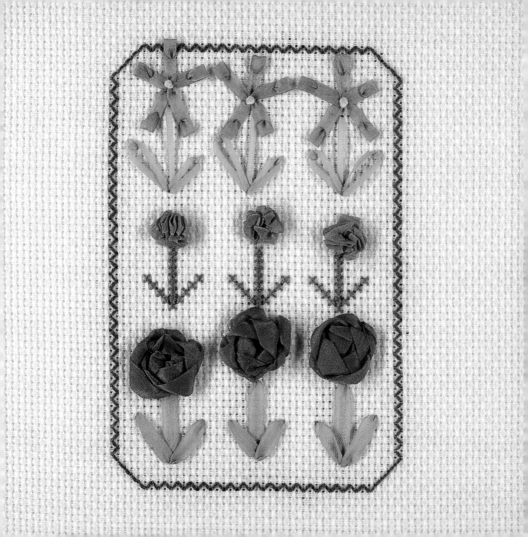

## Combined Lazy Daisy and Ribbon Stitch

Combining two separate embroidery stitches, both worked in embroidery ribbon, to make one 'new' stitch can give even more texture to the finished work. Almost any two stitches can be combined and here a Ribbon Stitch is worked over a Lazy Daisy Stitch.

To work a Combined Lazy Daisy and Ribbon Stitch, start by working the Lazy Daisy Stitch (see page 14) that will form the lower stitch. The centre of this stitch will be filled with the Ribbon Stitch so try to keep the loop of the stitch quite loose and open.

Once this stitch is complete, work a Ribbon Stitch (see page 10) in the centre. For this stitch, bring the needle through to the right side of the fabric at the base point of the Lazy Daisy Stitch, so that both stitches radiate out from the same point, and take the needle back inside the loop formed by the first stitch (see diagram).

The two separate elements of this combined stitch can either be worked in the same colour, or in contrasting or toning shades, and the widths of ribbon used can also be varied. Altering the length of the Ribbon Stitch can also change the final appearance of the combined stitch. However, it is best worked so that no base fabric is left visible inside the Lazy Daisy Stitch loop.

### Double Flower Diamond

The petals of these flowers are each worked as a Combined Lazy Daisy and Ribbon Stitch using two toning shades of 4mm Offray Embroidery Ribbon. One flower uses colour 183 for the Lazy Daisy Stitch, whilst the overlaid Ribbon Stitch is worked in colour 430. The other flower uses colours 467 and 178. The leaves are simple Lazy Daisy Stitch (see page 14) in 4mm ribbon, colour 564.

The design is completed in Anchor Stranded Cotton by working French Knots as the flower centres using colour 301, and a Stem Stitch outline in colour 877.

*Double Flower Diamond* A trace-off pattern for this design is on page 108.

## Satin Stitch

Satin Stitch worked with an embroidery ribbon can fill an area very quickly, giving a smooth surface, and it is worked in exactly the same way as if stranded cotton were being used.

Bring the needle through to the right side of the fabric, along one edge of the area to be filled, then take the needle back along the other side of the shape, leaving a strand of ribbon running right across the area. The next stitch is made in exactly the same way, bringing the needle up through the fabric next to the first point (see diagram).

As embroidery ribbon is much wider than stranded cotton, the distance between the end points of each stitch must be just less than the width of the ribbon being used, so that each strand of ribbon lays next to the previous one, overlapping very slightly so none of the base fabric shows. Take care that each strand of ribbon lays totally flat and is not twisted. Where the ribbon passes through the fabric, the ribbon will be pulled in at the ends of the stitches, leaving slight gaps at the edges of the area. To avoid this, use a fairly narrow embroidery ribbon.

When working Satin Stitch using an embroidery ribbon, it is vital that the fabric is held at the correct tension within an embroidery hoop or frame. Embroidery ribbons have less 'give' than other embroidery threads and if the fabric has been pulled too tight whilst in the frame or hoop, once it is removed the strands of ribbon forming each stitch will be too long and the embroidered area will sag away from the fabric.

### Pierced Heart

This heart is filled with Satin Stitch in 4mm Offray Embroidery Ribbon, colour 235, and outlined with a line of Back Stitch in Anchor Stranded Cotton, colour 46. The arrow is also worked in ribbon — but this time it is a metallic ribbon. The flight and point of the arrow are again worked in Satin Stitch using $^1/_{16}$in Kreinik Metallic Ribbon, colour 002HL, whilst the main section is worked as two lines of Straight Stitch using $^1/_8$in ribbon.

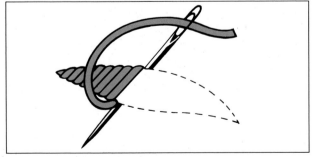

*Pierced Heart* A trace-off pattern for this design is on page 92.

## *Loop Stitch*

As its name suggests, Loop Stitch creates loops of ribbon that sit on the surface of the fabric. As each loop is only held in position by the base fabric weave, it is not a hardwearing stitch and is best used for items that will not be handled regularly.

To make a Loop Stitch, bring the needle through to the right side of the fabric at the required point. Holding the ribbon against the fabric, take the needle back through to the wrong side at the same point it emerged, until a small loop of ribbon is left on the right side (see diagram). Take

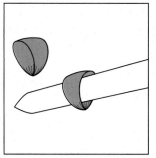

care that the ribbon does not twist so that the loop remains smooth.

When a design requires a series of Loop Stitches to be made, these will often need to be exactly the same size. To ensure every loop is identical, slip a knitting needle inside the loop of ribbon as it is tightened. Once the ribbon sits neatly around the knitting needle, it can then be removed. It may be a good idea to make a note of the size knitting needle you are using, so that should you stop and re-start your embroidery several days later, you will know exactly which size to use!

The resulting Loop Stitch will stand away from the fabric. If it is to lay to one particular side, a tiny securing stitch can be worked using embroidery thread. Position this stitch so that it does not show or spoil the shape of the loop, and work it through the underneath layer of the loop only. Working these securing

stitches will also make the stitch far more hardwearing.

**Scrolling Flower Border**
This scrolling design can be repeated to form a border. All the flower heads are worked as bands of Loop Stitch using 7mm and 4mm Offray Embroidery Ribbon, colours 260 and 660. The stems and flower-head bases are worked in Anchor Stranded Cotton, colour 267, as Stem Stitch and Satin Stitch respectively. The flower centres are worked as French Knots using stranded cotton, colour 306, and the leaves are Ribbon Stitch (see page 10) using 7mm ribbon, colour 570.

*Scrolling Flower Border* A trace-off pattern for this design is on page 96.

# Twisted Stem Stitch

Most styles of embroidery use Stem Stitch as the obvious choice to depict the stems of foliage or flowers within a design, and the same also applies to ribbon embroidery. However, if the ribbon is twisted as the stitches are made, the effect created looks even more natural, reflecting the nubbly texture of many creeping plants.

To work Twisted Stem Stitch, bring the needle through to the right side of the fabric at the beginning of the stitching line. Twist the needle and ribbon once or twice and

take the needle to the back of the fabric further along the line, ensuring the ribbon is twisted as it lays across the fabric. Bring the needle back to the right side midway along the first stitch, passing the needle to one side of the twisted ribbon, and make another stitch in the same way (see diagram). Continue in this way along the line, ensuring the needle always comes through the fabric at the same side of the previous stitch.

The effect created by a line of Twisted Stem Stitch can be varied greatly by the number of times the ribbon is twisted for each stitch. If a wide ribbon is used, the ribbon will begin to form a tube as it twists.

Although the ribbon should be twisted on the right side of the fabric, it is best to ensure that it always lays flat across the wrong side so that the finished work will also lay flat.

If the ribbon is twisted the same number of times for each stitch, the resulting line will be fairly evenly textured. However, the effect can be much more random — and natural — if the number of twists for each stitch is varied.

## Flower Tile

Reminiscent of Victorian tiles, this symmetrical floral design features Twisted Stem Stitch stems worked in 2mm Offray Embroidery Ribbon, colour 570. All the leaves and flower petals are Lazy Daisy Stitch (see page 14) using 4mm ribbon, in colours 570, 117 and 810. French Knots fill the centres of the flowers and these are worked using Anchor Stranded Cotton, colour 300.

*Flower Tile* A trace-off pattern for this design is on page 97.

## Straight Stitch Rose

A Straight Stitch Rose is very similar in appearance to the Ribbon Rose on page 16 but does not require the use of a second thread. It does, however, use more ribbon as the ribbon carries across the back of the work.

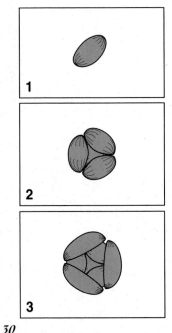

**1**

**2**

**3**

**Fig 1** To make a Straight Stitch Rose, begin by making one small Straight Stitch (see page 20) across the centre of the circle the rose is to fill.

**Fig 2** Now make three more Straight Stitches in a triangular shape surrounding this central stitch, leaving the ribbon fairly loose and allowing it to twist naturally. Position these stitches so that their ends meet and they cover the ends of the first central stitch.

**Fig 3** Work another triangular 'round' of Straight Stitch surrounding the previous set, positioning the ends of these stitches midway along the sides of the previous 'round'.

**Fig 4** Continue in this way, adding

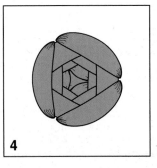

**4**

more triangular 'rounds' of Straight Stitch until the circle is filled, ensuring each 'round' of stitches overlaps the previous one. On the last 'round', position the ends of the stitches just under the edges of the previous set of stitches so that a circular shape is formed.

### Rose Swag

Any simple embroidered initial can be made really special by adding this swag beneath it. Start by working the stem of the swag as a Chain Stitch line using Anchor Stranded Cotton, colour 209. After this, work the Straight Stitch Roses using 7mm Offray Embroidery Ribbon, colour 447. The flower buds and leaves are worked in Straight Stitch (see page 20) using 4mm ribbon, colours 447 and 584. The initial is worked in Chain Stitch using stranded cotton, colour 109. Search through any old books or magazines you can find, or look on packets to find an initial you like and simply trace it from there, enlarging it as required.

*Rose Swag* A trace-off pattern for the swag is on page 97.

## *Padded Straight Stitch*

Extra surface texture can be added to ribbon embroidery by simply padding out an ordinary Straight Stitch. There are a variety of ways Padded Straight Stitch can be worked and what you choose will depend on the style of the embroidery and the effect to be created.

**Fig 1** If the stitch is only to be slightly padded, this can be achieved using stranded cotton. Work a couple of Straight Stitches centrally within the area to be covered. The ribbon Straight Stitch (see page 20) can then be worked over these stitches.

**Fig 2** If the stitch is to be quite large, the padding stitches can be worked as either French Knots or Bullion Stitch, again using stranded cotton. These will give the Padded Straight Stitch a full and firm texture.

If a soft effect is required, a soft knitting yarn can be used. Work one small stitch centrally over the area the ribbon will cover before working the ribbon Straight Stitch. This will give a soft but full Padded Straight Stitch.

If the final Padded Straight Stitch is to be short but very rounded — like a small ball or berry — the stitch can be simply padded using toy filling. Work the Straight Stitch but do not pull it tight. Tuck a very small amount of toy filling between the fabric and the ribbon and then tighten the ribbon around it.

### Blossom Tree

This stylised tree design has succulent leaves formed by working Padded Straight Stitch. Here the effect was achieved by working two big French Knots using Anchor Stranded Cotton, colour 266, under a simple Straight Stitch (see page 20) worked in 7mm Offray Embroidery Ribbon, colour 567. The blossom stems are Straight Stitch worked in 2mm ribbon, colour 563, with a French Knot at the end in stranded cotton, colour 972. The trunk and branches are lines of Twisted Stem Stitch (see page 28) worked in 4mm ribbon, colour 846.

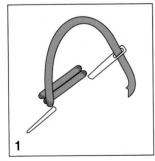

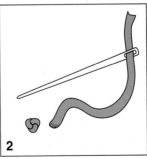

*Blossom Tree* A trace-off pattern for this design is on page 98.

## *Twisted Lazy Daisy Stitch*

Twisted Lazy Daisy Stitch is made in virtually the same way as Lazy Daisy Stitch (see page 14), but the ribbon loop is twisted, giving a thinner, more textured stitch. These twisted stitches make an ideal choice for a design that requires thin, angular leaves, stems of grass or twigs.

Any width of ribbon can be used for a Twisted Lazy Daisy Stitch — but a wider ribbon will give the stitch a more ruffled texture.

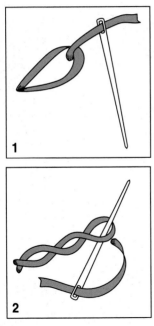

**Fig 1**   To make a Twisted Lazy Daisy Stitch, begin by working a Lazy Daisy Stitch (see page 14) to the point where the tying stitch is about to be completed, ensuring the ribbon loop is left fairly loose.

**Fig 2**   Slip the needle back through the first part of the stitch, leaving the ribbon loop free. Carefully twist the loop the number of times required and then thread the needle back through the loop. The tying stitch can then be worked and the stitch is completed.

The number of times the loop is twisted can be varied — the more times it is twisted, the thinner the final stitch will be. If the ribbon is twisted many times, the resulting stitch will become a thin 'tube' of ribbon.

## Tulip Circle

These tulips sit inside three rings of Stem Stitch worked in Anchor Stranded Cotton, colours 87, 226 and 110. The stems are single Straight Stitches (see page 20) worked in 2mm Offray Embroidery Ribbon, colour 581, with the leaves worked as Twisted Lazy Daisy Stitch in 4mm ribbon in the same shade. The flower petals are Lazy Daisy Stitch worked in 4mm ribbon, colours 178 and 463 alternately.

Although both the flower petals and leaves are worked using the same width of ribbon, twisting the loop twice for each leaf creates a much thinner stitch.

*Tulip Circle*  A trace-off pattern for this design is on page 95.

## *Knotted Ribbon Stitch*

A Knotted Ribbon Stitch is formed by replacing the little 'fold' at the end of a Ribbon Stitch (see page 10) with a knot. Although the same effect could be created by working a

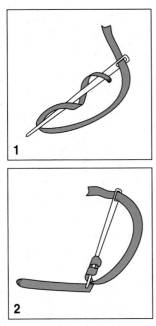

Straight Stitch with a French Knot at the end, this stitch works both elements at the same time.

**Fig 1** To make a Knotted Ribbon Stitch, bring the needle through to the right side of the fabric at the end of the stitch opposite the end where the knot is to be. Wind the ribbon twice around the point of the needle, as though making a French Knot.

**Fig 2** Lay the ribbon flat along the line of the stitch and insert the needle through the ribbon at the knot end of the stitch.

Holding the ribbon around the needle, gently pull the needle through the fabric and ribbon, forming the knotted end as the stitch is completed.

The number of times the ribbon is taken around the point of the needle can be increased to form a bigger knot and, if the knot is left fairly loose, the knotted end will appear more like a crumpled ball.

Although this stitch could, in theory, be worked with any width of ribbon, the best effect is achieved using very fine ribbon.

### Swirling Fronds

The feathery fronds of the side flowers of this design are created by Knotted Ribbon Stitch worked with 2mm Offray Embroidery Ribbon, colour 660. The swirling stems are lines of Chain Stitch in Anchor Stranded Cotton, colour 269. The central flower petals are Lazy Daisy Stitch (see page 14) worked in 4mm ribbon, colour 244, and the flower centre is a group of French Knots in stranded cotton, colour 42.

*Swirling Fronds* A trace-off pattern for this design is on page 98.

# Couched Ribbon

Taking a length of embroidery ribbon through the fabric many times can damage it and, when all that is required is a simple wavy line of ribbon, couching it in place is an obvious choice. The effect created will be that of one continuous line and the ribbon only needs to pass through the fabric at each end of the line.

To couch a length of ribbon, bring the ribbon through to the right side of the fabric at the beginning of the line it is to cover. If required, and to avoid any risk of damaging the ribbon, the end of the ribbon can be taken through to the wrong side, rather than pull the full working length to the right side. Thread a second needle with stranded cotton. Lay the ribbon along the line it is to cover and, using the second needle and thread, secure it in place with tiny stitches worked at even intervals across the width of the ribbon (see diagram).

When the end of the line to be covered is reached, take the ribbon back through to the wrong side and fasten off both the ribbon and the stranded cotton.

Within reason, a couched line can follow any shape. However, most embroidery ribbons are not very flexible and tend to fold rather than bend. Either use these folds as a style detail or use a thinner, more flexible ribbon.

If the line being followed is very shaped, the stitches over the ribbon will need to be placed very close together; similarly, the straighter the line the further apart the securing stitches can be.

## Celtic Knot

This continuous line of couched metallic ribbon recreates a classic Celtic knot. To give the design a regal look — and because metallic ribbon tends to be more flexible than 'silk' ones — it is worked using Kreinik $^{1}/_{8}$in Metallic Ribbon, colour 102, stitched in place with Anchor Stranded Cotton, colour 403.

When working this design, pass the ribbon alternately under and over areas already sewn in place. Start and end the ribbon at a point that will be covered by another piece of ribbon.

*Celtic Knot* A trace-off pattern for this design is on page 95.

38

## *Folded Loop Stitch*

Folded Loop Stitch uses both embroidery ribbon and matching embroidery thread and the effect it creates can be either smooth or highly textured. As this stitch has its loop secured to the fabric, it is much more hardwearing than an ordinary Loop Stitch.

To work a Folded Loop Stitch, begin by making a Loop Stitch (see page 26) using the embroidery ribbon. Now fold the loop of the stitch flat to form a point (see diagram) and lay this folded loop flat against the surface of the fabric. Using the embroidery thread, work a tiny stitch to secure the point of the fold to the fabric. The folded loop can be laid against the fabric in two ways: it can either be positioned so that the stitch is smooth, or so that a tiny 'cup' effect is formed.

Whilst the stitch worked to secure the loop to the fabric is usually a Straight Stitch, it can be varied depending on the effect to be achieved. The point of the Folded Loop Stitch can be accentuated by working a French Knot or it could even be secured by working another stitch using a fine embroidery ribbon.

### Flower Pot

Worked on Aida fabric, Folded Loop Stitch is used here to add texture to a simple Cross Stitch design.

Begin by working the areas in Cross Stitch using Anchor Stranded Cotton, colour 433. Using Back Stitch, outline the pot in the same shade and then work the stems using colour 226. The petals of the main flower are then added using 7mm Offray Embroidery Ribbon, colours 327 and 028, working Folded Loop Stitch, folded so that a tiny 'cup' is formed. The buds at the ends of the stems are also Folded Loop Stitch using one of the same ribbons — but this time the stitch has been laid against the fabric so that it is flat and smooth. The leaves are all worked in the same way as the buds using 4mm ribbon, colour 581.

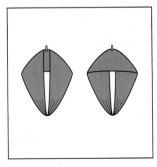

*Flower Pot* A chart for this design is on page 112.

# *French Knot*

A French Knot worked in embroidery ribbon creates a wonderful ruffled 'ball' of ribbon that can be used to great effect within an embroidery.

To work a French Knot, bring the needle through to the right side of the fabric at the required point. Wind the ribbon loosely around the point of the needle. Holding the ribbon firmly around the needle, twist the needle back on itself (see diagram), taking it back through to the wrong side of the fabric next to the point where it first emerged.

As embroidery ribbons are much bulkier than other embroidery threads, it is usually only necessary to wind the ribbon around the needle once or twice for each knot. Do not wind the ribbon around the needle too tightly as this can not only damage the ribbon but also make it very difficult to pull the needle through.

French Knots can be worked using any width of embroidery ribbon but they are most successful when one of the thinner widths is used.

## Sunflower Square

All the flower centres and the corner points of this design are worked as French Knots, using 2mm Offray Embroidery Ribbon, colour 030, for the sunflower and 4mm ribbon, colours 824 and 178, to work the other flowers. The sunflower petals are Ribbon Stitch (see page 10) in 4mm ribbon, colour 660, and the daisy petals are Straight Stitch in Anchor Stranded Cotton, colour 1. The square is formed with Couched Ribbon (see page 38) using 2mm ribbon, colour 567, and stranded cotton, colour 1025. The ladybird body is a Lazy Daisy Stitch (see page 14) worked in 4mm ribbon, colour 235. The dragonfly has Straight Stitch (see page 20) wings and body, worked in 4mm ribbon, colours 303 and 824. The body stripes are also in Straight Stitch, but the head is a French Knot, all worked in 2mm ribbon, colour 030.

The remaining detail on both bugs is worked in Straight Stitch and French Knots using stranded cotton, colour 403.

*Sunflower Square* A trace-off pattern for this design is on page 99.

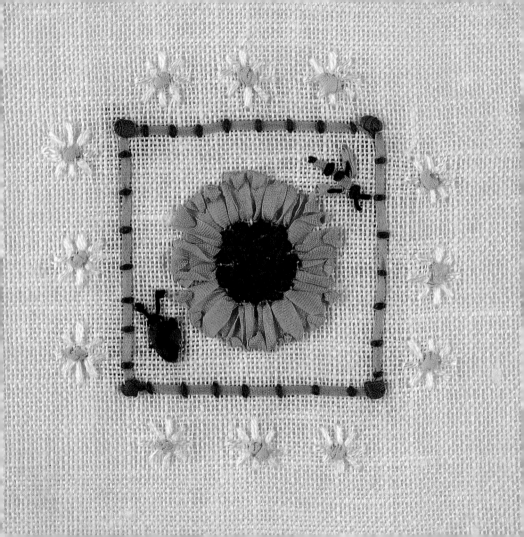

## Gathered Rosette

Tiny rosettes of ribbon can be attached to an embroidery to form single flower heads or large spots of textured colour; these rosettes are formed by gathering the edge of a short piece of ribbon.

The finished size of the Gathered Rosette will be twice the width of the ribbon used and they can be made using any soft wide ribbon — the length required for each rosette is roughly six to seven times the width of the ribbon.

Sometimes a small gap will remain in the centre — to fill this, another stitch, such as a French Knot, can be worked.

**Fig 1**  To make a Gathered Rosette, cut a piece of wide embroidery ribbon about 4–5cm (1$^1$/$_2$–2in) long. Using stranded cotton, work a line of tiny Running Stitches along one edge of the strip, positioning these stitches as close as possible to the edge of the ribbon.

**Fig 2**  Pull up the thread so that the ribbon gathers up and forms a circle. Fasten off the two ends of the thread securely. Position the rosette on the embroidery, tucking the ends of the ribbon under so that they do not show. Attach the Gathered Rosette with tiny stitches worked through both the fabric and the ribbon at the centre of the rosette. If required, tiny stitches can also be worked around the edge of the rosette.

### Butterfly

The large spots on the wings of this butterfly are Gathered Rosettes made using 7mm Offray Embroidery Ribbon, colours 235 and 327. French Knots (see page 42), made using 4mm ribbon, colours 327, 745 and 235, fill the centres of the rosettes and decorate the rest of the wings. The body of the butterfly is worked in Satin Stitch and the outline and antennae are worked in Stem Stitch — all worked using Anchor Stranded Cotton, colour 403. The French Knots at the ends of the antennae are worked using stranded cotton, whilst the eyes use 4mm ribbon, colour 030.

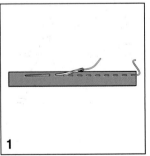

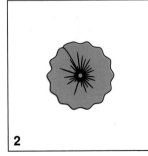

*Butterfly* A trace-off pattern for this design is on page 101.

## Ribbon Tufts

Attaching tiny tufts of ribbon to an embroidery will create a fringed effect. Bear in mind when usiing this stitch that the tufts are only held in place by the weave of the fabric and so are not particularly hardwearing.

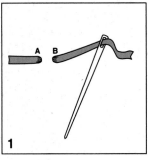

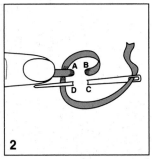

**Fig 1** To work a Ribbon Tuft, take the needle through the fabric at A, from the right to wrong side, and bring the needle back up at B. Pull the ribbon through the fabric, leaving a short end of about 2cm (³/₄in) on the right side.

**Fig 2** Hold the free end of the ribbon down and slide the needle under this strand. Take another stitch through the fabric from C to D, with the loop under the needle.

**Fig 3** Pull the ribbon through, so that the loop forms a 'knot' around the two ends, and trim the ends of the ribbon to the required length. A small stitch can be worked where the two ends pass over the loop to secure the tuft.

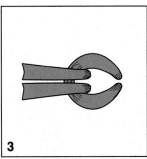

### Tufted Flower Whirl

The heads of these flowers are all formed with Ribbon Tufts, worked using 4mm Offray Embroidery Ribbon, colour 617. The stems on which they sit are worked as lines of Twisted Stem Stitch (see page 28) and the base of the flower heads are Lazy Daisy Stitch (see page 14), all worked using 4mm ribbon, colour 846. The leaves are then added by working long Folded Loop Stitch (see page 40) using 7mm ribbon, colour 567, secured with a tiny stitch worked using Anchor Stranded Cotton, colour 266.

*Tufted Flower Whirl* A trace-off pattern for this design is on page 99.

Ribbon embroidery works well when bright
colours and bold designs are used. These
items, from left to right, are a patchwork
cushion cover, a hearts and stripes pillow
and a tapestry milkmaid picture. The
instructions for making these items are on
pages 117–119.

## Combined Lazy Daisy and Bullion Stitch

The appearance of a plain Lazy Daisy Stitch can be altered greatly by changing the stitch that secures the loop to the fabric. Here a Bullion Stitch is worked, rather than a simple Straight Stitch.

When making the Bullion Stitch, wind the ribbon loosely around the needle as it will be difficult to pull the needle through if the coil is too tight. If a wide ribbon is being used, it may be easier to work the Bullion Stitch section with a narrower ribbon.

**Fig 1** To make a Combined Lazy Daisy and Bullion Stitch, begin by working a Lazy Daisy Stitch (see page 14) to the point where the tying stitch is about to be completed.

**Fig 2** Take the needle through the fabric on the other side of the loop, as though to complete the Lazy Daisy Stitch, and bring it back up again within the loop, next to the previous stitch. Do not pull the needle through yet. Now make the Bullion Stitch by winding the ribbon around the needle point several times and pulling the needle through the fabric, holding the coiled ribbon in place with the thumb. Still holding the coiled ribbon in place, take the needle to the back of the fabric on the other side of the loop.

### Heart Square

This simple heart motif would work well placed on the pocket of a garment — the square outline could easily be adjusted to the required size!

The outline of the heart is a simple line formed by French Knots (see page 42) made using 2mm Offray Embroidery Ribbon, colour 640. The central flower motif has Combined Lazy Daisy and Bullion Stitch petals and Lazy Daisy Stitch (see page 14) leaves, all worked using 4mm ribbon, colours 095 and 550. The square itself is worked as lines of Straight Stitch (see page 20) worked using 2mm ribbon, colour 028, with matching petals and knots in the corners.

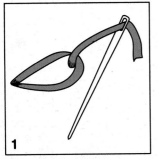

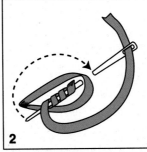

*Heart Square* A trace-off pattern for this design is on page 100.

## *Ruched Ribbon Lines*

Ruched strips of ribbon are a finishing touch often found on couture clothing and they work just as well within ribbon embroidery. Ruched Ribbon Lines are best worked with a fairly wide embroidery ribbon and the finished width of the ruched line is twice the width of the ribbon.

**Fig 1** To work a Ruched Ribbon Line, cut a strip of ribbon roughly three times the length of the line it is to cover. Using a matching shade of stranded cotton, fold under one end of the ribbon and secure the thread at A, stitching through both layers. Now work a zig-zag line of small Running Stitches along the entire length of the ribbon, positioning the 'points' of the line just next to the edge of the ribbon. At the end of the strip, tuck under the cut end and finish the stitching at B — do not fasten off the thread.

**Fig 2** Very carefully pull up the thread so that the strip measures the same as the line it is to cover. As the ribbon gathers up, tiny half rosettes will be formed either side of what is now a straight line of stitching. Once the strip is the correct length, fasten off the thread securely. Arrange the gathers evenly along the length of the strip and ensure it does not twist.

Position the strip over the line it is to cover. Using stranded cotton, stitch in place by stitching centrally along the strip.

### Gold Fish

The Ruched Ribbon Lines across the body of this fish are worked using 7mm Offray Embroidery Ribbon, colours 745 and 556, stitched in place with a line of Chain Stitch in matching Anchor Stranded Cotton, colours 314 and 238. The type of stitching used to attach the Ruched Ribbon Line depends on the effect to be created. A line of Running Stitch will leave the centre of the ribbon ruffled but a line of Chain Stitch will flatten the centre of the strip. The outline of the fish is worked in Stem Stitch and the eye is Satin Stitch, both worked using stranded cotton.

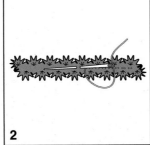

**1**

**2**

*Gold Fish* A trace-off pattern for this design is on page 101.

# Coral Stitch

The knotted effect of lines of Coral Stitch make it an ideal stitch to use to outline an embroidery. And, if the ribbon is left quite loose, an effect similar to luxuriant swags can be created!

To work a line of Coral Stitch, bring the needle through to the right side of the fabric at the beginning of the stitching line. Form a loop of ribbon around the point where the next stitch will be made and take a small stitch through the fabric at right angles to the line, passing the needle under the top strand of the loop but over the lower strand (see

diagram). Pull up the ribbon gently, easing the knot into position.

Continue along the line in this way, simply taking the needle through to the back of the fabric at the end of the line.

When working a continuous line of Coral Stitch, make the ends meet perfectly by working the last 'knot' over the beginning of the line and then taking the needle back to the wrong side under this knot.

Coral Stitch lines can be worked using any width of embroidery ribbon. With a very fine ribbon, the line will be smooth with knots scattered along its length. Working a Coral Stitch line in a wide ribbon will change its appearance — the lengths of ribbon between each knot will become ruffled and folded, giving a much more random effect.

Coral Stitch can be used for both straight and curved lines — the ease with which the line will bend around a curve will depend on the length of each stitch.

## Rose Mini-Sampler

This little sampler is worked mainly in Cross Stitch using Anchor Stranded Cotton, colours 1215, 1211 and 1207, but has interest added by working little details in ribbon.

The centres of the Cross Stitch roses are worked as Ribbon Roses (see page 16) using 7mm Offray Embroidery Ribbon, colour 168. The two little daisies, each made up of five Lazy Daisy Stitches (see page 14), either side of the word *Rosa* are worked in 2mm ribbon, colour 332.

The lines within the design are all worked in Coral Stitch, with 4mm ribbon being used for the frame and 2mm ribbon for the lines dividing the sections, both colour 168.

*Rose Mini-Sampler* A chart for this design is on page 113.

## Folded Rose

Life-like, full-blown roses can be recreated using embroidery ribbon by making a Folded Rose. This style of rose will stand away from the fabric but, as the ribbon is folded repeatedly, it is only truly successful if a wide ribbon is used.

**Fig 1** Cut a 25cm (10in) length of 7mm wide embroidery ribbon and thread a needle with matching colour stranded cotton. Starting at one end of the ribbon, fold the cut end over diagonally and then fold the point in. Make a stitch at the base of this rose centre to secure the ribbon.

**Fig 2** Fold the free end of the ribbon to the back and then fold the first section onto the free end, roughly aligning the top of the first section with the edge of the ribbon. Make another stitch at the base to secure the folds.

Continue in this way, folding the free end to the back and then the worked section over onto the free end, until the complete length of ribbon has been used. Secure the free end at the back, behind the folded petals. The Folded Rose is now complete and can be attached in the required position.

Although this rose is a little tricky to get the hang of first time, it is well worth practising as the effect created is quite spectacular.

### Rose Bouquet

Five Folded Roses form the centre of this bouquet. Each rose is made using 7mm Offray Embroidery Ribbon, colours 168, 095 and 140, and they are attached after all the other embroidery has been worked.

Begin with the stems worked in Stem Stitch using Anchor Stranded Cotton, colour 214, then add in the Lazy Daisy Stitch (see page 14) leaves in 2mm and 4mm ribbon, colours 564, 513 and 530. Work the French Knots (see page 42) using 2mm ribbon, colour 645. Finally the Folded Roses can be attached.

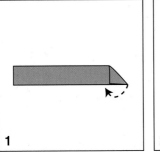

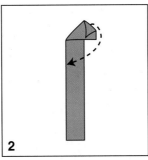

*Rose Bouquet* A trace-off pattern for this design is on page 102.

## *Fly Stitch*

Individual Fly Stitches worked using an embroidery ribbon appear totally different from those worked in a stranded cotton as the twists and folds of the ribbon create a heavily textured stitch. Fly Stitch can be used singly or in rows.

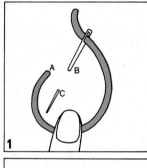

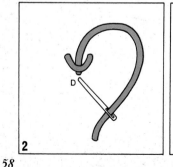

**Fig 1** To work a Fly Stitch, bring the needle through to the right side of the fabric at A. Make a stitch by inserting the needle level with and to the right of point A, at point B, holding down the loop of ribbon with the thumb. Bring the needle back up again at C (below and midway between A and B), bringing the needle through the ribbon loop.

**Fig 2** Complete the stitch by taking the needle through the fabric at D, directly below C, securing the ribbon loop with this stitch.

**Fig 3** If points C and D are very close together, the completed stitch forms a V-shape. However, this can be changed to a Y-shape by increasing the distance between C and D.

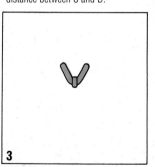

### Good Egg

This Fabergé-style egg has the outline and band across it worked in Coral Stitch (see page 54) using Kreinik 1/8in Metallic Ribbon, colour 002HL. The scattered decoration over the egg is formed by working Fly Stitch using the same metallic ribbon in a narrower 1/16in width.

As each Fly Stitch is made, the ribbon can either be left to twist and fold naturally as here, so that each stitch will be totally unique, or it can be kept flat, creating a more streamlined effect.

*Good Egg* A trace-off pattern for this design is on page 106.

## *Feather Stitch*

Feather Stitch, worked in fine embroidery ribbon, can be used to form branching lines of stems within a floral design or on its own to form a folk-art style border and it is worked in a very similar way to Fly Stitch (see page 58).

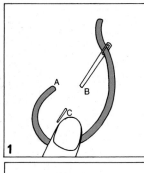

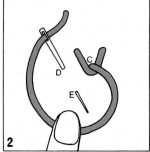

**Fig 1** To work a line of Feather Stitch, start by making a Fly Stitch (see page 58) to the point where the second part of the stitch is about to be completed.

**Fig 2** Holding the loop of ribbon down with the thumb, take the needle through the fabric at D — points C and D are level and the same distance apart as A and B. Bring the needle back through the fabric and loop at E — as with a Fly Stitch, this point is below but midway between the previous two points.

**Fig 3** Continue along the line in this way, alternately making stitches to each side. Complete the last stitch by taking the needle back through the fabric on the other side of the final loop.

### Flower Bower

This floral design is a combination of six separate stitches, all worked using Offray Embroidery Ribbon. In the centre is a Ribbon Rose (see page 16) worked in 7mm ribbon, colour 095. All the flower buds comprise three Lazy Daisy Stitches (see page 14) using 4mm ribbon, colours 571 and 095. Five tiny Lazy Daisy Stitches in 2mm ribbon, colour 303, make up the blue flowers, each of which has a French Knot (see page 42) centre worked in 2mm ribbon, colour 617. The remaining leaves and stems are worked in 2mm ribbon, colour 571, as a mixture of Straight Stitch (see page 20), Lazy Daisy Stitch, Fly Stitch (see page 58) and Feather Stitch.

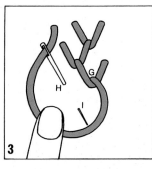

*Flower Bower* A trace-off pattern for this design is on page 103.

# Woven Ribbon

Filling an area within an embroidery with Woven Ribbon will recreate perfectly the appearance of a basket. Depending on the style of the embroidery, toning or contrasting colours can be used to form a checkerboard effect.

To fill an area with Woven Ribbon, begin by working Satin Stitch (see page 24) over the area. Position each stitch so that the ribbon does not overlap, leaving a very tiny gap between each strand, and ensure that the ribbon lays totally flat against the fabric.

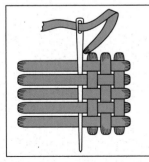

Work another set of Satin Stitch at right angles to the first set. Bring the needle through to the right side of the fabric at the required point and then weave the needle alternately under and over the ribbons of the previous set of stitches. Pull the ribbon through the ribbon lattice-work and smooth out the work so that the ribbons are all laying totally flat. Take the needle back through to the wrong side of the fabric and begin the next stitch. With this stitch, take the needle under the strand of ribbon that the previous stitch went over and vice versa to form the woven effect (see diagram). Continue in this way until the area is completely covered with Woven Ribbon.

Using different colours of ribbon for each of the two sets of stitches will create a checkerboard effect. However, as embroidery ribbon has a sheen that makes the colour look slightly different depending on how the light catches it, the Woven Ribbon area will still have a very slight checkerboard effect even if the same colour is used for all the stitching.

To accurately convey the appearance of a woven basket, try using a finer width ribbon for the vertical set of stitches than was used for the horizontal set.

## Flower Tub

The tub at the base of these flowers is filled with Woven Ribbon, worked in two toning shades of 4mm Offray Embroidery Ribbon, colours 824 and 810. The stems are worked in Chain Stitch using Anchor Stranded Cotton, colour 861. All the leaves are Lazy Daisy Stitch (see page 14) worked in 4mm ribbon, colour 587, whilst the flowers are Ribbon Stitch (see page 10) in 4mm ribbon, colours 434, 435 and 467.

*Flower Tub* A trace-off pattern for this design is on page 105.

## Knot Couched Ribbon

Lengths of embroidery ribbon can be couched on to the fabric by working a series of knots, rather than stitches, along the ribbon (see Couched Ribbon, page 38). This method of couching will give a much softer look than Couched Ribbon as the ribbon can twist and turn naturally and is just held in place at selected points along its length.

To work a line of Knot Couched Ribbon, cut a length of ribbon and lay this over the line it is to cover, allowing it to twist and turn naturally. If necessary, pin the ribbon

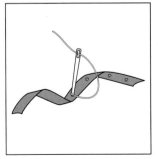

in place. Thread a needle with stranded cotton and, beginning near one end of the ribbon, bring the needle through to the right side midway across the ribbon and make a small French Knot (see page 42). Continue along the length of ribbon in this way (see diagram), making French Knots centrally across the ribbon at intervals of about 12mm (½in).

The cut ends of the ribbon can either be left free on the surface of the embroidery or taken through to the wrong side.

Take care not to flatten any naturally occurring twists or folds in the ribbon by positioning the knots so that they fall on either side of the folds and twists.

As embroidery ribbons are usually folded around a card, it is advisable to iron the length of ribbon before it is attached – ironing it after it has been attached will turn the soft folds into hard creases!

## Bluebirds and Bow

These bluebirds are worked in Satin Stitch in Anchor Stranded Cotton, colour 1033. The French Knot eye and Straight Stitch beak (see page 20) are also worked in stranded cotton, colours 403 and 292.

To form the bow section, cut a 35cm (14in) length of 7mm Offray Embroidery Ribbon, colour 303, and tie a bow at the centre, making 5–6cm (2–2½in) loops and trimming the ends to 8–9cm (3–3½in).

Position the bow on the fabric and stitch in place behind the knot. Attach the remaining length of ribbon with French Knots worked in stranded cotton, colour 1033.

*Bluebirds and Bow* A trace-off pattern for this design is on page 105.

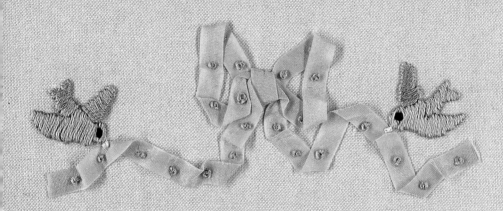

## *Crossover Loop Stitch*

Crossover Loop Stitch is very similar in appearance to Loop Stitch (see page 26) but is made in the same sort of way as Ribbon Stitch (see page 10). As the ribbon is split when the stitch is made, it is also slightly more hardwearing than Loop Stitch.

To work a Crossover Loop Stitch, bring the needle through to the right side of the fabric at the base of the stitch. Twist the ribbon as shown in the diagram to create a loop and then take the needle back through to the wrong side a little distance away from

where it emerged, passing the needle through the centre of the ribbon. Gently ease the ribbon through the fabric so that a twisted loop is left on the surface.

If a number of Crossover Loop Stitches of the same size are to be worked, insert the point of a knitting needle into the loop before pulling the ribbon through. Tightening the stitch around this will ensure all the loops are the same size.

To create a different effect, the ribbon can be twisted more times before the needle is returned through the fabric.

## Lily Swirl

Worked on Aida fabric, this design combines Cross Stitch and ribbon embroidery. As with all designs of this type, begin by working the background Cross Stitch areas, starting with the central lily in Anchor Stranded Cotton, colours 1028, 76 and 1021. Add in the Back Stitch lines using stranded cotton, colour 210. Once all these areas have

been completed, the ribbon embroidery can be worked. The centre of the lily is Straight Stitch (see page 20) worked in 2mm Offray Embroidery Ribbon, colour 169. Work the leaves in Lazy Daisy Stitches (see page 14) using 2mm ribbon, colour 580, then add in the Straight Stitch flower stems using the same ribbon. The upper and lower flower tufts are groups of Crossover Loop Stitch worked in 4mm ribbon, colour 140, whilst the single flower tufts along the stem use the same width ribbon in colour 215.

*Lily Swirl* A chart for this design is on page 116.

## *Lazy Daisy Stitch with Knotted End*

A Lazy Daisy Stitch can be used to create a leaf unfurling by making a simple knot — like one you would tie in the end of a piece of string — in the ribbon forming the stitch that holds the loop in place. Similar in many ways to a Combined Lazy Daisy and Bullion Stitch (see page 50), the end of this stitch is a softer knot and it is easier to work.

To make a Lazy Daisy Stitch with Knotted End, begin by working a Lazy Daisy Stitch (see page 14) to the point where the tying stitch is about to be completed. Make a loose

single knot in the ribbon, positioning this knot against the fabric at the point where the ribbon emerged (see diagram). Now complete the stitch in the usual way, leaving the knot covering the end of the loop of the stitch.

To make the stitch look even more like a real leaf, allow the ribbon to twist and turn as the loop is formed. This, combined with the loose knot, will make the leaf appear as though it is just about to uncurl.

This stitch is best worked in a fairly wide embroidery ribbon so that the twists and turns will be apparent. It can, however, be successfully worked in a narrow ribbon but the effect created will be totally different, with the loop section being much thinner and the knot more apparent.

Another way of varying the appearance of this stitch is to use different widths and colours of ribbon for each part of the stitch. Try using a wide ribbon in one colour for the

loop section of the stitch and a toning or contrasting colour of ribbon in a narrower width for the knot section.

### Cornflowers

All the leaves of this design have been worked as Lazy Daisy Stitches with Knotted Ends to give them a realistic appearance. First the stems are worked in Chain Stitch using Anchor Stranded Cotton, colour 210. Then all the leaves are added using 4mm Offray Embroidery Ribbon, colour 580. Add the flower petals in Lazy Daisy Stitch (see page 14) using 2mm or 4mm ribbon, colour 327, and then the centres which are groups of French Knots (see page 42) using 2mm ribbon, colour 660.

*Cornflowers* A trace-off pattern for this design is on page 104.

## *Folded Stitch*

Folded loops of ribbon can be used as an alternative to some of the other, more textured ribbon embroidery stitches when a smoother effect is required. Here, the loops lay flat against the fabric.

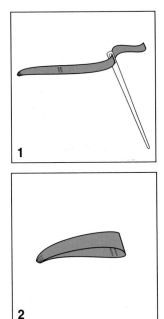

**Fig 1** To make a Folded Stitch, bring the needle through to the right side of the fabric at one end of the stitch and lay the ribbon flat along the line of the stitch. Using a matching colour of stranded cotton, make two or three tiny Straight Stitches across the width of the ribbon at the point where the fold will be. These stitches secure the folded end of the ribbon.

**Fig 2** Fold the ribbon back over these securing stitches so that they do not show and take the ribbon back through to the wrong side of the fabric at the same point it emerged, leaving just a flat, folded loop of ribbon on the surface of the embroidery.

### Harvest Posy

This posy combines traditional freestyle embroidery with ribbon embroidery. Begin by working Satin Stitch leaves and Stem Stitch flower stems in Anchor Stranded Cotton, colour 681.

Add in the stalks of the ears of corn, again in Stem Stitch, using stranded cotton, colour 306. The blue flowers are worked in Lazy Daisy Stitch (see page 14) in 2mm Offray Embroidery Ribbon, colour 345, whilst the leaves on these stems are Ribbon Stitch (see page 10) worked in 4mm ribbon, colour 563. The main daisy petals are all Folded Stitch in 4mm ribbon, colour 028, with the centres worked as French Knots (see page 42) in 2mm ribbon, colour 745. The ears of corn are also Folded Stitch, made using 4mm ribbon, colour 660, but these have an extra Straight Stitch worked over the folded end, in stranded cotton, colour 306.

*Harvest Posy* A trace-off pattern for this design is on page 106.

## Twisted Straight Stitch

Although most ribbon embroidery stitches require the ribbon to be kept smooth and flat over the surface of the fabric, some stitches achieve their particular effect by twisting the ribbon as the stitch is made. Twisted Straight Stitch is one such stitch.

To make a Twisted Straight Stitch, bring the needle through to the right side of the fabric and lay it flat over the fabric. Now twist the ribbon as many times as required, ensuring this twisted section falls over the line of the stitch. Take the needle back through

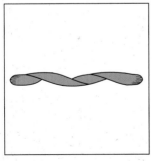

to the wrong side, keeping the twists of the ribbon on the fabric surface (see diagram).

The number of twists made for each stitch can be varied. One twist will simply create a 'turn' in the ribbon, whilst many twists will make the ribbon form a tiny hollow tube that will sit on the surface of the fabric.

To continue to twist the ribbon further will cause the tube to buckle and 'worm'.

The number of twists made within each stitch will also depend on the length of the stitch and the width of ribbon being used. A wide ribbon will not normally allow the same number of twists to be made had narrow ribbon been used. The same effect can be created by twisting the ribbon twice for a short stitch and four times for a stitch twice as long.

If a group of Twisted Straight Stitches are to be made, ensure the ribbon is twisted the same number of times for each stitch so that they all match.

### Snowflakes

Simple snowflakes worked in a metallic ribbon could be scattered over a cushion cover or bedspread to create a stunning winter look.

All these snowflakes are made using Kreinik Metallic Ribbon, colour 001HL. Both $1/8$ in and $1/16$ in ribbon has been used for the French Knots (see page 42), whilst Straight Stitch (see page 20) has only been worked with the narrower ribbon. The wider ribbon has been used for Twisted Straight Stitch and for each stitch the ribbon has been twisted twice.

*Snowflakes* A trace-off pattern for this design is on page 107.

## Knotted Loop Stitch

A Knotted Loop Stitch is worked in a similar way to a Folded Loop Stitch (see page 40) but the embroidery ribbon loop is knotted.

To work a Knotted Loop Stitch, bring the needle through to the right side of the fabric at the point where the stitch will be attached to the fabric. Make a single knot in the ribbon — the sort you would tie in a piece of string — and position this knot so that it falls at the other end of the stitch, when the ribbon is laid flat. Keeping the ribbon flat against the fabric, take the needle back through to the

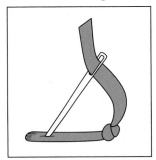

wrong side (see diagram) near to where it emerged, piercing the previous strand of ribbon with the needle. Pull the ribbon through gently so that the knot in the ribbon falls at the end of the stitch.

If desired, the loose knotted end of the stitch can be secured to the fabric by working two or three tiny stitches in a matching shade of stranded cotton, positioning these stitches so that they are hidden from view by the knot.

Tying a knot in the ribbon makes the complete stitch a crumpled loop of ribbon, adding texture to what is otherwise a fairly smooth stitch. The knot can either be pulled tight or left quite loose, depending on the effect to be achieved.

As the knot forces the ribbon to fold, creating the crumpled effect, this stitch is best worked in a wide embroidery ribbon. If narrow ribbon is used, the effect will be similar to that of a Knotted Ribbon Stitch (see page 36).

### Dandelions

These flowers are formed by working a ring of Knotted Loop Stitch, leaving the knots all quite loose. For the petals use 7mm Offray Embroidery Ribbon, colour 745, and fill the centres with loose French Knots (see page 42) worked in 4mm ribbon, colour 780. The stalks are worked in Stem Stitch in Anchor Stranded Cotton, colour 209, and the leaves are Lazy Daisy Stitch (see page 14) in 4mm ribbon, colour 584.

*Dandelions* A trace-off pattern for this design is on page 110.

74

## *Twisted Ribbon Stitch*

A totally different look can be given to a simple Ribbon Stitch (see page 10) by twisting the embroidery ribbon whilst the stitch is being worked. A Twisted Ribbon Stitch is made in virtually the same way as a flat Ribbon Stitch except the ribbon does not have to be kept flat.

To work a Twisted Ribbon Stitch, bring the ribbon through to the right side of the fabric. Now twist the ribbon many times until it forms a soft 'tube' of ribbon and lay this 'tube' over the stitch line. Take the needle back through to the

wrong side of the fabric, inserting the needle through the ribbon tube (see diagram). Ease the ribbon through the fabric gently, leaving a little bunched 'knot' at the end of the stitch. Take care not to pull too firmly or this bunched 'knot' will slip through to the wrong side.

This stitch can be worked with any width of embroidery ribbon. When the finest, 2mm, ribbon is used, the main part of the stitch will form a very fine line, making this stitch ideal for the antennae of a butterfly or the stamens of a flower centre. Whatever width of ribbon is used, the main part of the stitch will usually end up roughly half as wide as the ribbon that was used.

Whilst this stitch is usually worked with the ribbon twisted many times, it can be successfully worked with just one or two twists. The effect will be much softer and more textured, making it ideal for depicting flower petals, leaves or blades of grass.

## Framed Flower

A simple cross stitch motif such as this would be ideal to use on a small mat or coaster — or it could be repeated along a runner or across the bottom of a curtain.

Worked on an even weave fabric, this design uses just Cross Stitch and Twisted Ribbon Stitch. Start by working all the Cross Stitch areas using Anchor Stranded Cotton, colours 681 and 20. Once these are complete, work the petals of all the flowers in Twisted Ribbon Stitch using 7mm Offray Embroidery Ribbon, colour 260.

*Framed Flower* A chart for this design is on page 115.

Pastel and floral designs lend themselves to ribbon embroidery as these pretty items show. From left to right, you have an embroidered purse for jewellery or handkerchiefs, an embroidered pillowcase, a miniature photograph frame mount and a baby's pinafore with an embroidered yoke. The instructions for these items are on pages 120–124.

# *Whipped Running Stitch*

Whilst it is quite difficult to embroider a curved line using embroidery ribbon alone, working these shaped lines as Whipped Running Stitch will give the smooth effect required.

To work a line of Whipped Running Stitch, begin by threading a needle with stranded cotton which matches the colour of the ribbon. Using this thread, work along the line in Running Stitch, making each stitch just slightly longer than the width of ribbon that will be used for the whipping

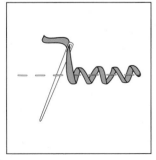

stitches. Fasten off the ends of this thread securely as the ribbon will 'pull' against them.

Thread a needle with embroidery ribbon, then bring this needle through to the right side of the fabric at one end of the line of Running Stitch. Slide the needle under the first Running Stitch, ensuring it does not catch the fabric, and pull the ribbon through gently. Allow the ribbon to twist as it wants. Continue along the line in this way (see diagram), sliding the needle under each Running Stitch from the same side. At the end of the line, take the needle through to the wrong side and fasten off.

## Bird and Heart

The outline of this heart is Whipped Running Stitch, worked using Anchor Stranded Cotton, colour 110, and 4mm Offray Embroidery Ribbon, colour 463. The bird itself is worked in Stem Stitch in stranded cotton, colours 110, 88 and 301. The tail feathers and flower petals are worked in Lazy Daisy Stitch (see page 14) using 4mm ribbon, colours 183 and 463.

The flower centres, bird's eye and all other spots are French Knots (see page 42) worked in 2mm ribbon, colours 645, 584 and 463.

Whilst the outline of this heart shape uses matching shades of embroidery ribbon and stranded cotton, different and interesting effects can be created by using toning or contrasting colours, or varying widths of ribbon, and also if the base Running Stitches are placed further apart.

*Bird and Heart* A trace-off pattern for this design is on page 103.

# Combined Lazy Daisy and Straight Stitch

Working a Combined Lazy Daisy and Straight Stitch can create a two-colour flower petal that can add extra interest and realism to an embroidery.

To work a Combined Lazy Daisy and Straight Stitch, begin by working a Lazy Daisy Stitch (see page 14) using the first colour of embroidery ribbon. This part of the stitch is best worked using a fairly wide ribbon so that no fabric remains visible along the centre of the stitch.

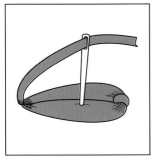

Using the second colour of ribbon, bring the needle through to the right side of the fabric at the base of the Lazy Daisy Stitch and make a Straight Stitch (see page 20) over the Lazy Daisy Stitch, taking the needle back through the ribbon of the previous stitch (see diagram).

The length of this stitch can be varied according to the effect required, but it must pierce the ribbon of the previous stitch to hold that stitch closed, with no fabric showing.

The width of the ribbon used for this stitch can also be varied, but it should not be wider than the one used for the Lazy Daisy Stitch. If it is wider, it may cover the edges of the first stitch, thereby spoiling the two-colour effect.

Whilst this stitch is, obviously, most effective when two colours of ribbon are used, it will, of course, work just as well if both parts of the combined stitch are the same colour.

## Pansies

All these pansies are worked in the same way — it is just the colours that vary. The back pair of petals are ordinary Lazy Daisy Stitch (see page 14) in 4mm Offray Embroidery Ribbon. Over these petals, the remaining three petals are worked as Combined Lazy Daisy and Straight Stitch using 4mm ribbon.

The pansies are worked in colours 169, 640, 463 and 244, and each flower centre is a French Knot (see page 42) in 2mm ribbon, colour 030. All the pansies sit on stalks of Stem Stitch worked in Anchor Stranded Cotton, colour 210.

*Pansies* A trace-off pattern for this design is on page 102.

## Crossed Lazy Daisy Stitch

When working a standard Lazy Daisy Stitch (see page 14), the two ends of the loop part of the stitch pass through the fabric at the same point. However, if these two ends are moved apart, a totally different effect can be achieved. A Crossed Lazy Daisy Stitch has the ends of this loop stitch a little distance apart so that the loop crosses itself.

To make a Crossed Lazy Daisy Stitch, bring the needle through to the right side of the fabric. Take the needle back through the fabric a little distance away from where it

emerged, ensuring that the ends of the loops of ribbon cross over each other slightly (see diagram). Bring the needle up through the fabric and ribbon loop and complete the stitch in the same way as for a standard Lazy Daisy Stitch (see page 14).

Varying the length of the stitch in relation to how far apart the ends of the loop are placed can greatly alter the finished appearance of the stitch. A long stitch with the end points close together will appear very similar to a standard Lazy Daisy Stitch, whilst a short stitch with the ends wide apart will be totally different.

This stitch will work successfully in most widths of embroidery ribbon and can be used to form petals, buds or leaves.

### Aquarium

These golden fish are just single Crossed Lazy Daisy Stitch worked in 4mm Offray Embroidery Ribbon, colour 753. To accentuate their tails, a tiny Straight Stitch (see page 20) has been worked over the point where the stitch crosses the ribbon, using Anchor Stranded Cotton, colour 324. The eyes of the fish are tiny French Knots (see page 42) worked in stranded cotton, colour 403. The sand is formed by working Straight Stitch (see page 20) in 4mm ribbon, colour 645, and the seaweed is Twisted Stem Stitch (see page 28) using 2mm ribbon, colour 584. The bubbles are French Knots (see page 42) in 2mm ribbon, colour 028.

*Aquarium* A trace-off pattern for this design is on page 104.

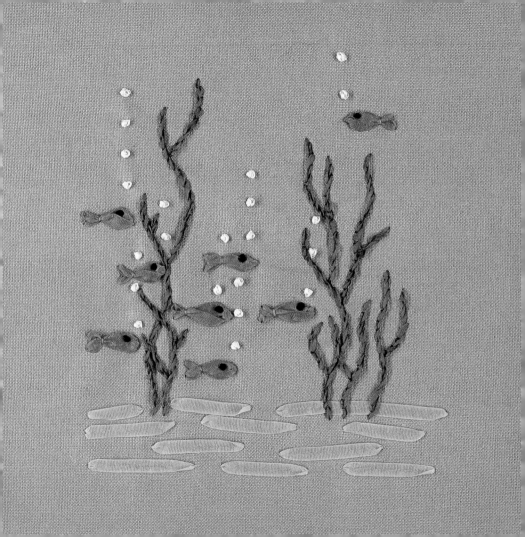

## *Bullion Stitch*

Bullion Stitch is frequently used in freestyle embroidery where it is worked in a stranded cotton. It can also be made successfully using a fine embroidery ribbon, although a little extra care needs to be taken.

To work a Bullion Stitch, bring the needle through to the right side of the fabric at one end of the stitch. Take the point of the needle through to the wrong side at the other end of the stitch and bring it back up next to the point it first emerged — do not pull the needle through. Wind the ribbon around the point of the needle

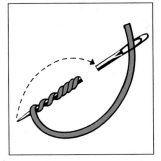

needle as many times as required (see diagram) and, holding this 'coil' of ribbon around the needle with the thumb, gently pull the needle through the fabric and 'coil'. Complete the stitch by taking the needle back to the wrong side next to the point it went down through the fabric previously.

The number of times the ribbon is wound around the needle will depend on the length of the stitch and the thickness of the ribbon. However, it is not normally necessary to wind the ribbon around the needle as many times as if the stitch were being worked in another, finer embroidery thread. No matter how many times the ribbon is wound round the needle, do not wind it too tightly as this will make it very difficult to pull the needle through.

### Tyrolean Flowers
The centres of most of these flowers are worked in Bullion Stitch using 2mm Offray Embroidery Ribbon, colours 640 and 028. The central area of the centre flower is completely covered with Bullion Stitch, whilst a pair of Bullion Stitches, positioned next to each other, form the centres of the smaller flowers. All the petals and leaves are Lazy Daisy Stitch (see page 14) in either 2mm or 4mm ribbon, colours 580, 327, 235 and 028, and the stems are worked in Chain Stitch in Anchor Stranded Cotton, colour 210. French Knots (see page 42) have also been worked using 2mm ribbon, colours 327, 235 and 640.

*Tyrolean Flowers* A trace-off pattern for this design is on page 110.

## *Stem Stitch Rose*

Another way of forming a rose within ribbon embroidery is by working it in Stem Stitch. This rose will lay quite flat against the surface of the fabric and is best worked using one of the thicker embroidery ribbons. However, if the rose is to be very small, it could be worked in a fine 2mm width ribbon.

To work a Stem Stitch Rose, start by bringing the needle through to the right side of the fabric near the centre of the circle to be filled by the rose. Make one short Straight Stitch (see page 20) across the centre of the circle, bringing the

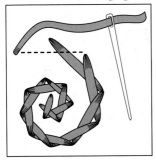

needle back up through the fabric to one side of this central stitch. Now work out from this point in a spiral of Stem Stitch, making the length of each stitch about twice the width of the ribbon and ensuring the needle always comes back up through fabric on the side of the previous stitch nearest the centre of the circle (see diagram).

As each stitch is worked, do not pull the ribbon through too tightly but allow it to twist or fold as it wants, to create natural-looking petals. When the circle has been filled, complete the rose by taking the needle back through the fabric under one of the previous 'petals'.

### Flower Square

The Stem Stitch Roses in this design have been worked in 4mm Offray Embroidery Ribbon, colours 140 and 215. All the other flowers, buds and leaves are worked in Lazy Daisy Stitch (see page 14)

using either 2mm or 4mm ribbon, colours 564, 430 and 215. The centres of the daisies are French Knots in 2mm ribbon, colour 617, whilst the flower stems are Stem Stitch in Anchor Stranded Cotton, colour 877. The two square outlines are worked in Coral Stitch (see page 54) in 4mm ribbon, colour 564.

A Stem Stitch Rose like those shown here could easily be substituted within a design for either a Ribbon Rose (see page 16) or a Folded Rose (see page 56), and vice versa. It is simply a case of working the rose you find easiest and that best suits the look you are trying to create.

*Flower Square* A trace-off pattern for this design is on page 109.

# Embroidery Ribbons for Cross Stitch and Tapestry

Whilst embroidery ribbons are most commonly used within freestyle embroidery and to add detail to a piece of Cross Stitch, there is no reason why they cannot be substituted for the threads used for a tapestry or Cross Stitch design. The effect they create will be totally different to that formed by the other threads and can add greatly to the finished appearance of the work.

Any time that embroidery ribbons are to be substituted for another thread, the ribbon chosen should roughly equal the thickness of the thread it is to replace. As an approximate guide only, 2mm Offray Embroidery Ribbon can be substituted for two or three strands of stranded cotton, in both Cross Stitch and needlepoint designs. A 4mm ribbon would be suitable to replace an Anchor Tapisserie Wool. Whatever thread is to be replaced, the only way to be sure that the substitute will correctly cover the canvas or fabric is to try out several alternatives by working a few stitches on a small scrap of fabric or canvas first. Once you are happy with the effect created, simply substitute the selected ribbon for the thread or wool stated.

When a ribbon is chosen as a substitute for either a Cross Stitch or tapestry design, the stitches worked with it are done in exactly the same way as if stranded cotton was being used. Ribbons do have a tendency to twist as they lay across the fabric, so it is purely a matter of personal choice whether you decide to ensure every stitch lays flat or is allowed to twist and turn.

## Milkmaid

Within this Cross Stitch design, the cow has been worked using 2mm Offray Embroidery Ribbon, colours 030 and 028. The effect created, as the stitches twist and turn, helps to recreate the short curly 'fur' of the cow.

Worked on a 14 count Aida fabric, all the remaining Cross Stitch areas are worked in two strands of Anchor Stranded Cotton, colours 24, 130, 132, 355 and 6, and Kreinik Metallic Fine (#8) Braid, colours 025 and 202HL.

Extra details, such as the milkmaid's apron straps and the footstool, have been added as Straight Stitch (see page 20) and the eyes of the cow are French Knots (see page 42).

*Milkmaid* A chart for this design is on page 114.

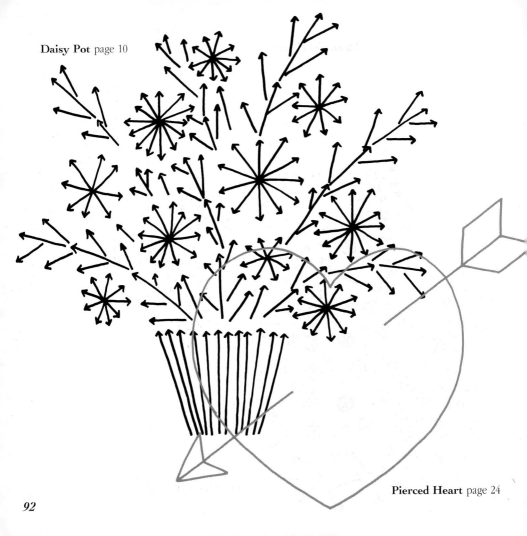

**Daisy Pot** page 10

**Pierced Heart** page 24

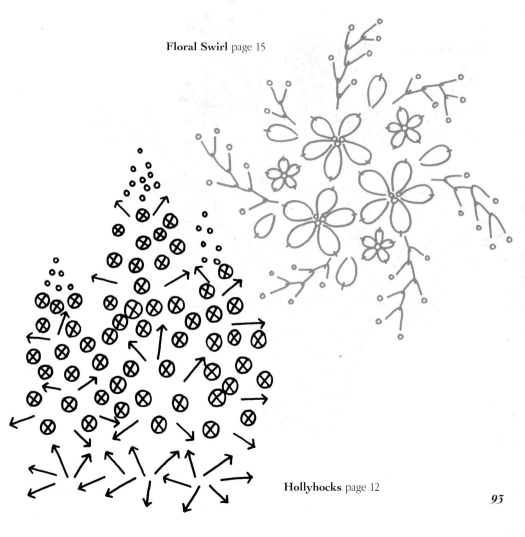

**Floral Swirl** page 15

**Hollyhocks** page 12

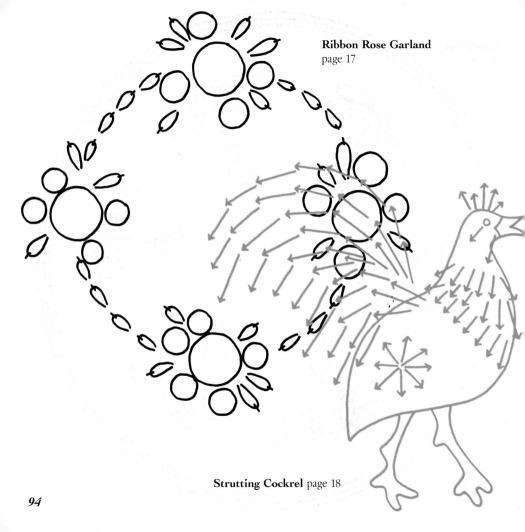

**Ribbon Rose Garland**
page 17

**Strutting Cockrel** page 18

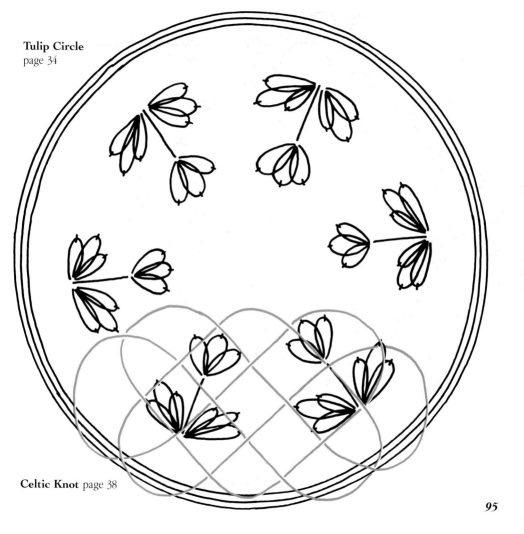

**Tulip Circle**
page 34

**Celtic Knot** page 38

95

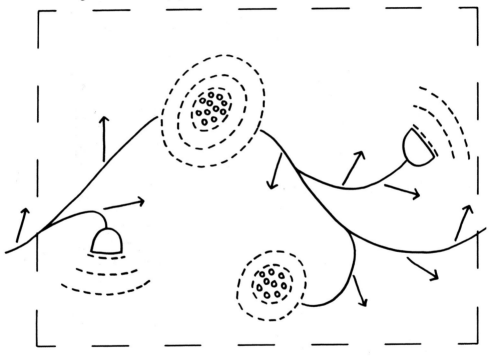

**Flower Tile**
page 28

**Rose Swag** page 30

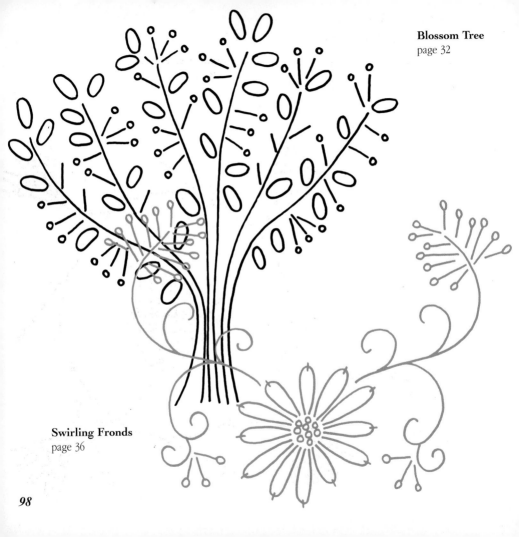

**Blossom Tree**
page 32

**Swirling Fronds**
page 36

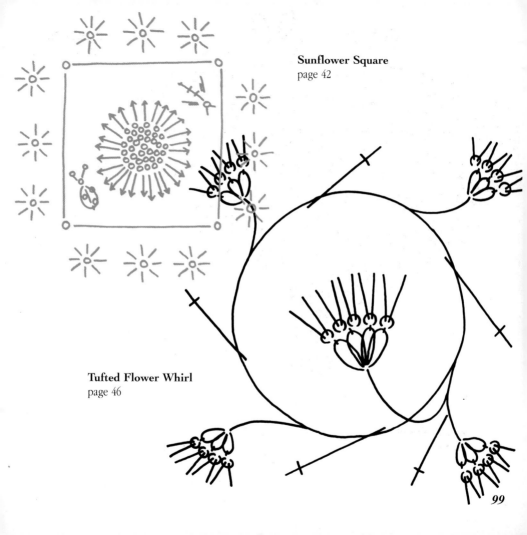

**Sunflower Square**
page 42

**Tufted Flower Whirl**
page 46

**Heart Square**
page 50

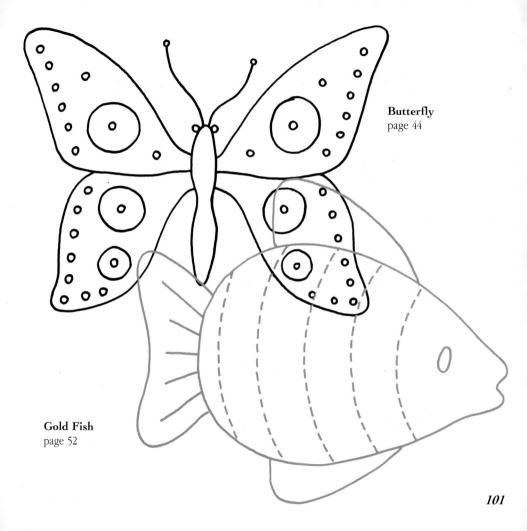

**Butterfly**
page 44

**Gold Fish**
page 52

*101*

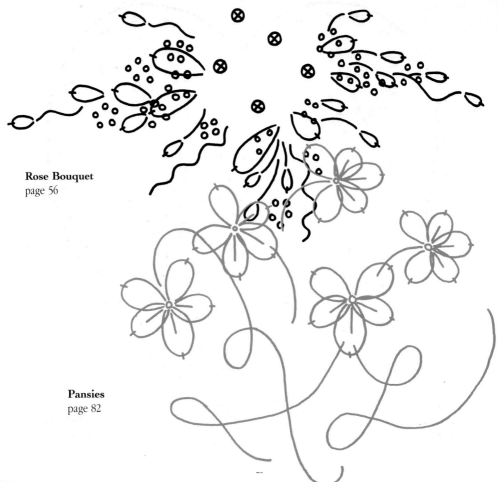

**Rose Bouquet**
page 56

**Pansies**
page 82

Above
**Bird and Heart**
page 80

**Flower Bower**
page 60

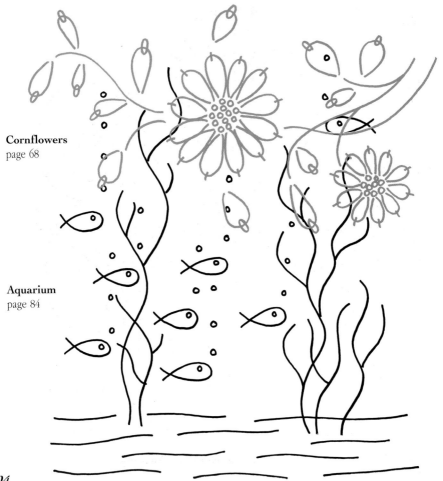

**Cornflowers**
page 68

**Aquarium**
page 84

**Flower Tub**
page 62

**Bluebirds and Bow** page 64

105

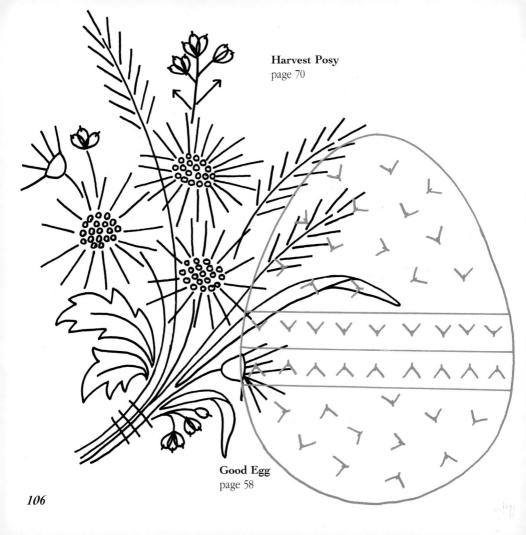

**Harvest Posy**
page 70

**Good Egg**
page 58

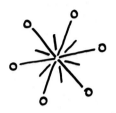

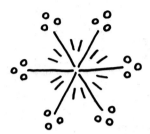

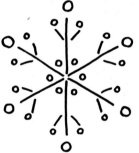

**Snowflakes**
page 72

**Double Flower
Diamond**
page 22

**Flower Square**
page 88

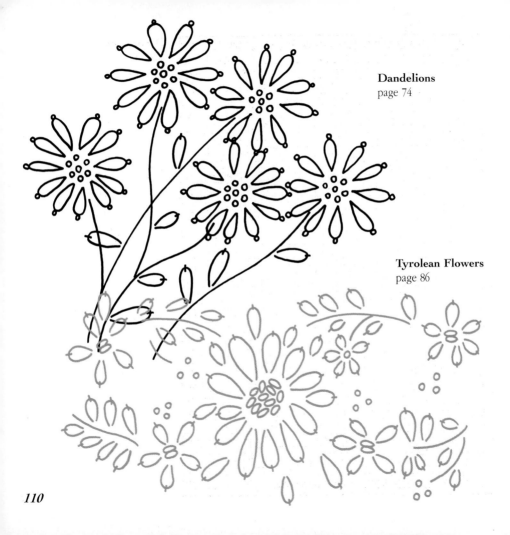

**Dandelions**
page 74

**Tyrolean Flowers**
page 86

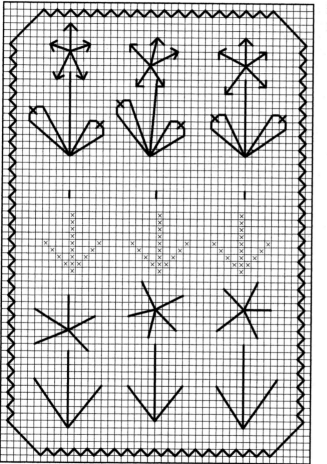

**Flower Pot**
page 40

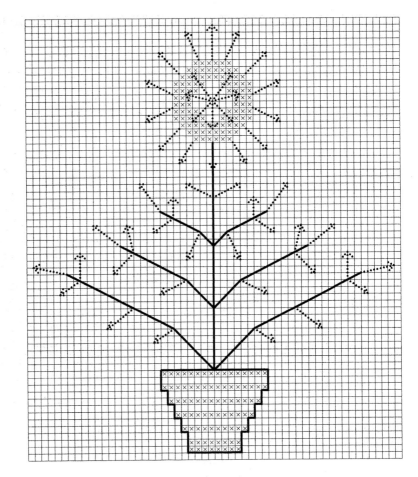

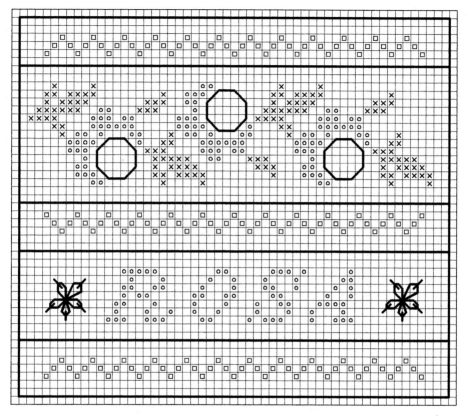

**Rose Mini-Sampler**
page 54

**Key**   Anchor Stranded Cotton

□ = 1215

☒ = 1211

○ = 1207

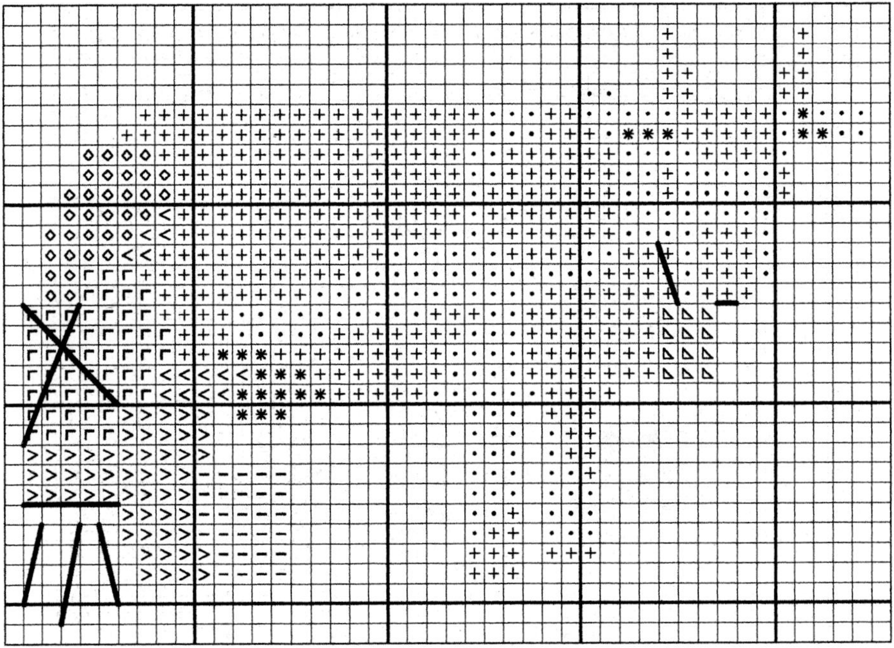

**Milkmaid**
page 90

**Key**

| | |
|---|---|
| + = 030 | } 2mm Offray Embroidery Ribbon |
| • = 028 | |

| | |
|---|---|
| * = 24 | |
| ⌐ = 130 | |
| > = 132 | } Anchor Stranded Cotton |
| ◇ = 355 | |
| < = 6 | |

| | |
|---|---|
| ◹ = 025 | } Kreinik Fine Braid (#8) |
| – = 202HL | |

**Framed Flower**
page 76 →

**Key** Anchor Stranded Cotton

| | |
|---|---|
| ☒ = 681 | |
| ○ = 20 | |

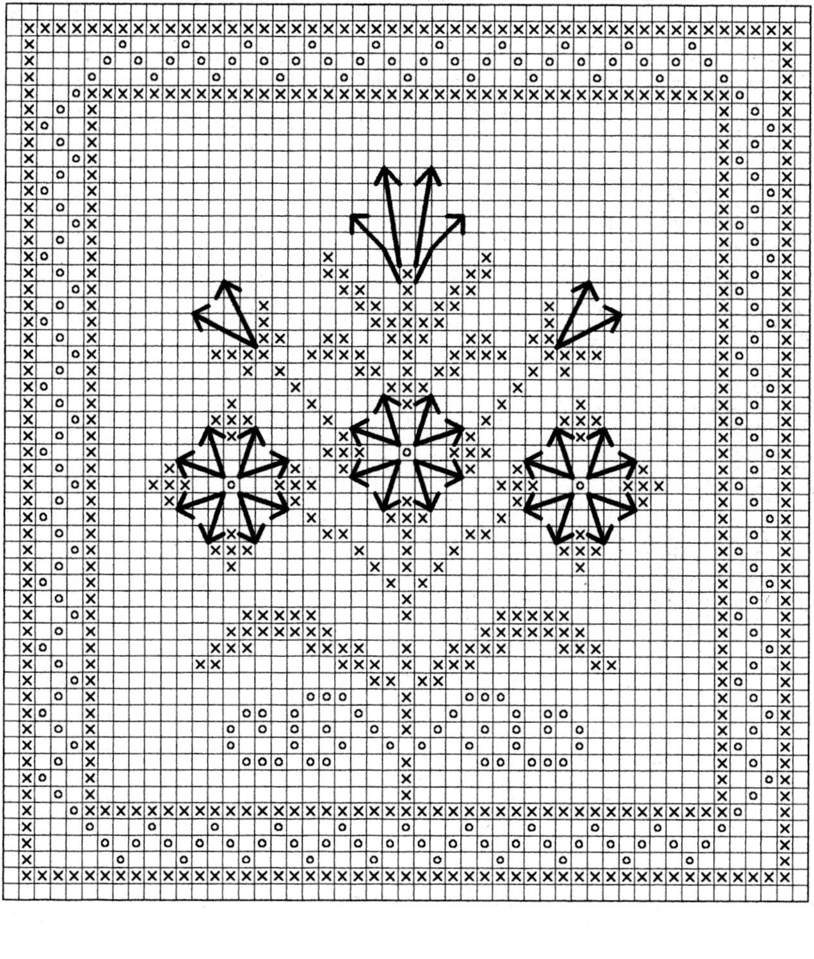

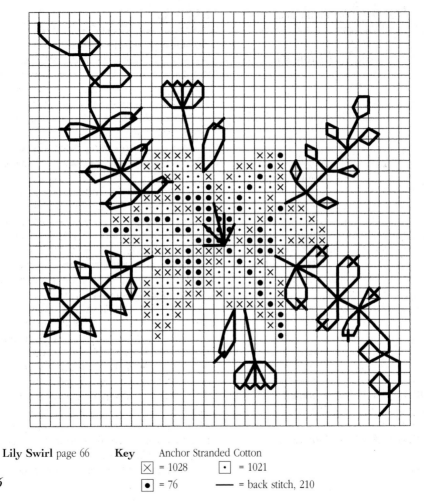

**Lily Swirl** page 66    **Key**    Anchor Stranded Cotton

| | | |
|---|---|---|
| ☒ = 1028 | ⊡ = 1021 | |
| ⬤ = 76 | — = back stitch, 210 | |

*Project Instructions* for the items shown on pages 48 and 49, 78 and 79, and 122 and 123.

## *Hearts and Stripes Pillow* shown on pages 48–49

### Measurements
Finished pillow is 24cm (9in) square (excluding frill)

### Materials
- 30cm (12in) square of cream fabric
- 30cm (12in) of 90cm (36in) wide striped fabric for border
- 30cm (12in) of 90cm (36in) wide checked fabric for frill and pillow back
- 4mm Offray Embroidery Ribbon: 1 card of Poppy 235 and Grass Green 584
- 2mm Offray Embroidery Ribbon: 1 card of Mandarin Orange 745 and Aegean Blue 327
- Matching sewing thread
- 24cm (9in) square cushion pad

### Working embroidery
Following trace-off pattern on page 100, work design centrally on the cream fabric , using the stitches given on page 50 and following colours:
**4mm Offray Embroidery Ribbon**
| | |
|---|---|
| Combined Lazy Daisy and Bullion Stitches | 235 |
| Lazy Daisy Stitches | 584 |

**2mm Offray Embroidery Ribbon**
| | |
|---|---|
| French Knots | 745 |
| Running Stitch | 327 |

### Making up
Seam allowance of 1cm ($^1/_3$in) is included.

Positioning design centrally, trim embroidered section to 14cm (6 $^3/_4$in) square. From striped fabric, cut four pieces 26cm x 8cm (10 $^1/_4$ x 3in) for border. From checked fabric, cut a 26cm (10 $^1/_4$in) square for pillow back and then cut and join 9cm (3 $^1/_2$in) wide strips to form one length of 190cm (75in) for frill.

With right sides together, pin one striped fabric strip to one edge of embroidered section, with striped strip extending beyond embroidered section for 7cm (2 $^3/_4$in) at both ends. Stitch pieces together, starting and stopping stitching 1cm ($^1/_3$in) in from edges of embroidered section. Join other three striped strips to embroidered section in same way. Press seams away from embroidered section and fold ends of striped strips so that corners of border appear mitred. Stitch in place.

Join ends of checked fabric frill to form a large loop. Press seam open. Fold loop in half, right sides outermost, so that raw edges meet at one side and other edge of loop is a fold. Press. Run gathering threads along raw edge and pull up to fit outer edge of pillow front. Matching raw edges and distributing gathers evenly, stitch frill to right side of pillow front.

Place pillow back over front and frill pieces, right sides together, and stitch along outer edges, leaving an opening. Turn right side out and press. Insert pad and stitch opening to close.

## *Milk Maid Picture* shown on pages 48–49

### Measurements
Finished embroidery measures 16.6 x 13cm (6 ½ x 5in)

### Materials
- 35cm (14in) square of Anchor 10 count Interlock Canvas
- 4mm Offray Embroidery Ribbon: 2 cards of Black 030, 1 card of Antique White 028 and 1 card of Blended Bronze 846
- Anchor Tapisserie Wool: 3 skeins of Sand 9522, 1 skein each of Cyclamen 8434, Chestnut 9566, Terracotta 8252, Ancient Blue 8734 and Ancient Blue 8742
- Kreinik Heavy (#32) Braid: 1 spool each of Antique Gold 221 and Grey 025
- Backing board, mount and picture frame to fit embroidery

### Working embroidery
Following Milkmaid chart on page 114, embroider design centrally onto canvas, using ribbons/threads and colours as given right and working entire design in Half Cross Stitch. When working embroidery, leave the stitches worked using embroidery ribbon fairly loose so that the canvas is covered.

### Offray Embroidery Ribbon
| | |
|---|---|
| Black patches on cow | 030 |
| White areas on cow | 028 |

### Anchor Tapisserie Wool
| | |
|---|---|
| Cow's udder and ears | 8434 |
| Milkmaid's hair | 9566 |
| Milkmaid's face and hand | 8252 |
| Milkmaid's blouse | 8734 |
| Milkmaid's skirt | 8742 |

### Kreinik Metallic Heavy (#32) Braid
| | |
|---|---|
| Cow bell | 221 |
| Bucket | 025 |

Once all these areas are complete, fill in background using Anchor Tapisserie Wool, colour 9522.

Complete the design by working the Straight Stitch and French Knot details: using Anchor Tapisserie Wool, work Straight Stitch at nose in colour 8434, French Knot eyes on cow in colour 8734, and Straight Stitch straps on milkmaid's back in colour 8742.

Using Kreinik Metallic Heavy (#32) Braid, colour 221, work Straight Stitch cow bell chain at neck. Using 4mm Offray Embroidery Ribbon, colour 846, work Straight Stitches to form milkmaid's stool.

When the embroidery has been completed, mount and frame as required.

# Patchwork Cushion Cover
*shown on pages 48–49*

## Measurements
To fit 40cm (15 ½ in) square cushion pad

## Materials
- 55cm (21 ½ in) of 90cm (36in) wide cream fabric
- 20cm (8in) of 90cm (36in) wide printed fabric
- 45cm (17 ½ in) of 90cm (36in) wide fabric for cushion back and piping
- 45cm (17 ½ in) square of fabric to back embroidery
- 1.80m (71in) of narrow piping cord
- 4mm Offray Embroidery Ribbon: 1 card each of Poppy 235, Grass Green 584, Mandarin Orange 745 and Aegean Blue 327
- 2mm Offray Embroidery Ribbon: 1 card each of Poppy 235, Grass Green 584, Mandarin Orange 745 and Aegean Blue 327
- Anchor Stranded Cotton: 1 skein each of Scarlet 46, Tangerine 314 and Lido Blue 433
- Matching sewing thread

## Working embroidery
From the cream fabric, cut out one 30cm (12in) square and four 25cm (10in) squares. Following Bird and Heart trace-off pattern on page 103, embroider full design centrally onto the larger fabric square, using stitches as given on page 80 and colours as follows:

### Anchor Stranded Cotton
| | |
|---|---|
| Heart and bird outlines | 46 |
| Outer wing | 314 |
| Inner wing | 433 |

### 4mm Offray Embroidery Ribbon
| | |
|---|---|
| Lower left and top right flower petals | 327 |
| Top left flower petals | 745 |
| Top three tail feathers | 584 |
| Lower two tail feathers | 745 |
| Heart outline | 235 |

### 2mm Offray Embroidery Ribbon
| | |
|---|---|
| Blue flower centres | 745 |
| Yellow flower centres | 235 |
| Bird's eye | 327 |
| Spots on bird | 584 |

All other French Knots all four shades, using colours at random

Using the same colours as given above, embroider the bird *only* centrally onto the four smaller fabric squares, reversing the design for two pieces.

## Making up
Seam allowance of 1cm (³/₈ in) is included on all pieces.

Positioning designs centrally, trim embroidered heart and bird square to 20cm (8in) square, and four small bird squares to 13cm (5in) squares.

From print fabric, cut out four pieces 20 x 13cm (8 x 5in). From embroidery backing fabric, cut a 42cm (11 ¹⁄₂ in) square. From cushion back fabric, cut two pieces 30 x 42cm (12 x 16 ¹⁄₂ in). Cut remainder of this fabric to make 4cm (1 ¹⁄₂ in) wide bias strips. Join these bias strips to make one piece 1.80m (71in) long.

With right sides facing, join one long edge of two print fabric rectangles to the sides of the large embroidered section. Join the side edges of two small embroidered squares to the short edges of one print fabric rectangle; repeat with last two embroidered squares and print rectangle. Ensure that all four birds face inwards. Press all seams open.

With right sides facing and matching seam lines, join all three strips to form one large square, ensuring birds are all the right way up. Press seams open.

With wrong sides facing, lay this patchwork square flat onto the embroidery backing square and tack both pieces together around outer edge.

Fold 2cm (³⁄₄ in) to wrong side along one long edge of both cushion back pieces, turn under raw edge and stitch in place. With right sides of both pieces uppermost, lay the two back pieces flat with the finished edges overlapping so that they form a 42cm (11 ¹⁄₂ in) square. Tack pieces together along the overlapping outer edges.

Wrap bias strip around piping cord and stitch as close as possible to cord to secure. Trim fabric so there is a 1cm (³⁄₈ in) seam allowance on the piping trim.

Lay embroidered cushion front flat with right side uppermost, pin and tack piping trim to outer edge, matching raw edges. Overlap ends of piping trim to neaten and snip into seam allowance at corners. With right sides facing, cover front with cushion back pieces, tack then stitch around all four edges, enclosing piping in seam. Trim corners, neaten seam and turn cushion cover right side out. Press. Insert cushion pad.

## *Violets Pillowcase* shown on pages 78–79

### Measurements
Embroidered panel measures approximately 10cm (4in) square

### Materials
- White cotton pillowcase
- 4mm Offray Embroidery Ribbon:
  1 card each of Grape 463 and Ultra Violet 467
- 2mm Offray Embroidery Ribbon:
  1 card of Daffodil 645
- Anchor Stranded Cotton: 1 skein of Winter Green 876

## Working embroidery

Following Pansies trace-off pattern on page 102, embroider design in top corner of pillowcase, using stitches as given on page 82 and colours as follows:

**Anchor Stranded Cotton**

All stems                                            876

**4mm Offray Embroidery Ribbon**

Lazy Daisy Stitch sections of all petals    463
Straight Stitch of front petals                  467

**2mm Offray Embroidery Ribbon**

Flower centres                                      645

Position motif as required — photograph shows the design approximately 10cm (4in) in and 13cm (5in) down from the corners. If making a pair, reverse design for the second pillowcase.

## *Baby's Embroidered Pinafore*
*shown on pages 78–79*

### Measurements
Embroidered motif measures approximately 13 x 6cm (5 x 2 ½ in)

### Materials
- Baby's pinafore with plain yoke
- 7mm Offray Embroidery Ribbon: 1 card of Blue Vapor 303
- Anchor Stranded Cotton: 1 skein each of Sea Blue 1033, Black 403 and Buttercup 292

## Working embroidery

Following the Bluebirds and Bow trace-off pattern on page 105, embroider design centrally onto the yoke, using stitches and colours as given on page 64.

## *Miniature Photograph Frame Mount* *shown on pages 78–79*

### Measurements
To fit a picture frame with an aperture of at least 11cm (4 ¼ in) square. The photograph aperture is approximately 5cm (2in) square

### Materials
- 25cm (10in) square of pale green fabric
- 4mm Offray Embroidery Ribbon: 1 card each of Tea Rose 140, Soft Blush 215 and Celadon 564
- 2mm Offray Embroidery Ribbon: 1 card each of Baby Maize 617 and Celadon 564
- Purchased photograph frame with aperture of at least 11cm (4 ¼ in) square
- Mount board to fit frame
- Fabric adhesive

### Working embroidery

Following Flower Square trace-off pattern on page 109, embroider outer section only of design centrally onto fabric, using stitches as given on page 88 and colours as follows:

Ribbon embroidery is ideally suited to convey all sorts of flowers. Here are, from left to right, flowers on a mat, dandelions on a spectacle case, a sunflower and daisies on a notebook cover and a framed picture of cornflowers, corn ears and daisies. The instructions for these are on pages 125–127.

**4mm Offray Embroidery Ribbon**

| | |
|---|---|
| Both square outlines | 564 |
| Daisy petals | 215 |
| Corner roses | 140 |

**2mm Offray Embroidery Ribbon**

| | |
|---|---|
| Leaves | 564 |
| Daisy centres | 617 |

## Making up

Trim the mount board so that it fits the photograph frame. Cut a 5.5cm (2 ¹/₈ in) square aperture centrally in the mount board. Lay the embroidery flat, wrong side uppermost, and place mount board onto fabric, ensuring that the design is placed centrally. Trim edge of the fabric back to within 2cm (³/₄ in) of mount board. Fold the fabric over to the back of mount board and secure it with glue. Cut hole in centre of the fabric and trim away excess to within 2cm (³/₄ in) of edges of central hole in mount board. Very carefully cut out to the corners. Fold fabric to wrong side of board and secure with glue. Assemble mount in the frame.

## *Embroidered Handkerchief or Jewellery Purse* shown on pages 78–79

### Measurements

Finished purse measures 14 x 20cm (6 ¹/₂ x 8in)

### Materials

- 60 x 30cm (24 x 12in) piece of peach fabric
- 7mm Offray Embroidery Ribbon: 1 card of Carnation 095
- 4mm Offray Embroidery Ribbon: 1 card each of Dark Moss 571 and Carnation 095
- 2mm Offray Embroidery Ribbon: 1 card each of Carnation 095, Dark Moss 571, Blue Vapor 303 and Baby Maize 617
- Anchor Stranded Cotton: 1 skein of Carnation 25
- 45 x 25cm (17 ¹/₂ x 10in) piece of fabric for lining
- Same size piece of 2oz synthetic wadding
- 1m (39 ¹/₂ in) of shiny narrow cord
- One button
- Matching sewing thread

### Working embroidery

Following Flower Bower trace-off pattern on page 103, embroider design centrally onto fabric, approximately 10cm (4in) above one short end of fabric, using stitches and colours as given on page 60.

### Making up

Make a paper pattern for the purse: draw a 38 x 20cm (15 x 8in) rectangle and divide into sections by marking lines across this rectangle at 14cm (5¹/₂in) and 10cm (4in) from each shorter end. The 10 x 20cm (4 x 8in) section forms flap, with remaining two 14 x 20cm (5½ x 8in) sections forming front and back of purse. Curve corners of flap section by drawing around the edge of a small saucer. Add 1cm (³/₈in) seam allowance on all edges. Using pattern cut out shape from embroidered fabric section, positioning embroidery centrally on flap. Cut out same shape from wadding and lining fabric.

Lay wadding out flat and cover with embroidered section, right side uppermost. With right sides facing, place lining onto embroidered section. Stitch all three together around outer edges, leaving an opening. Trim and snip seam and turn right side out. Stitch opening closed. Press carefully. Fold 14cm (5½in) front section of purse up towards back and flap sections, with right sides of lining together. Hand stitch side edges of back and front together. Attach cord around entire outer edge of flap, sides and base (fold) of purse, forming a button loop at base of flap. Attach button to correspond with cord loop.

## Cornflower Picture *shown on pages 122–123*

### Measurements
Embroidered design measures approximately 11 x 13cm (4 ¼ x 5 in)

### Materials
- 30 x 40cm (12 x 15 ½ in) piece of natural linen fabric
- 4mm Offray Embroidery Ribbon: 1 card each of Willow 563, Antique White 028 and Yellow Gold 660
- 2mm Offray Embroidery Ribbon: 1 card each of Venetian Blue 345 and Mandarin Orange 745
- Anchor Stranded Cotton: 1 skein each of Olive Green 681, Off White 2 and Antique Gold 306
- Backing board, mount and picture frame

### Working embroidery
Following the Harvest Posy trace-off pattern on page 106, embroider design centrally onto the fabric, using stitches and colours as given on page 70. When the embroidery has been completed, mount and frame as required.

## Notebook with Embroidered Cover *shown on pages 122–123*

### Measurements
Embroidered design measures approximately 8cm (3in) square

### Materials
- Hardback notebook
- Piece of beige fabric same size as book

when opened, plus 5-10cm (2-4in) on all edges
- 4mm Offray Embroidery Ribbon: 1 card each of Buttermilk 824, Rose 178, Yellow Gold 660, Poppy 235 and Blue Vapor 303
- 2mm Offray Embroidery Ribbon: 1 card each of Black 030 and Spring Moss 567
- Anchor Stranded Cotton: 1 skein each of White 1, Geranium 1025 and Black 403
- Fabric adhesive

## Working embroidery

Open notebook and place centrally onto fabric. Using lines of tacking stitch, mark spine and book outline on fabric. Following Sunflower Square trace-off pattern on page 99, embroider design on fabric in position required on front section of book, using stitches and colours as given on page 42.

## Covering book

Apply a very thin layer of adhesive over outer cover of book and wrap embroidered fabric around book, matching tacked lines to outer edges and spine. Remove tacking. When glue has dried, trim excess fabric to leave a margin of 2–3cm ($^3/_4$–1 $^1/_4$in). Cut vertically through fabric margin where spine meets front and back. Apply adhesive to wrong side of these fabric 'tabs' and tuck inside spine. Open book and glue fabric margins to inside of cover, mitring corners. Apply adhesive to page of

book facing inside cover and glue this page over raw edges of fabric.

## *Mat* shown on pages 122–123

### Measurements

Finished mat measures 30 x 45cm (12 x 17 $^1/_2$in)

### Materials

- 50 x 65cm (20 x 25 $^1/_2$in) piece of cream fabric
- 32 x 47cm (12 $^1/_2$ x 18 $^1/_2$in) piece of backing fabric
- 4mm Offray Embroidery Ribbon: 1 card of Antique White 028
- 2mm Offray Embroidery Ribbon: 1 card each of Emerald 580, Aegean Blue 327, Poppy 235, Lemon 640 and Antique White 028
- Anchor Stranded Cotton: 1 skein of Laurel Green 210
- Matching sewing thread

### Working embroidery

Using lines of tacking stitches, mark a 30 x 45cm (12 x 17 $^1/_2$in) rectangle on cream fabric to form outline of cloth. Mark another line across fabric 6cm (2 $^1/_2$in) in from both shorter edges and mark centre point of these lines. Following Tyrolean Flowers trace-off pattern on page 110, transfer central flower and the eight leaves radiating out from this flower only centrally over marked centre point. Now transfer full design onto fabric at both sides of this central flower to give a band of embroidery approximately 26cm (10 ¼ in) long. Embroider design using stitches and colours as given on page 86.

## Making up

Lay embroidered section flat, right side uppermost, and cover with backing fabric. Stitch the two pieces together along marked outline of cloth, leaving an opening. Trim seam, clip corners and turn mat right side out. Hand stitch seam opening closed. Press carefully, placing seam along outer edge. Top stitch through all layers 6mm (¼ in) in from all four edges of finished cloth.

## *Spectacle Case* shown on pages 122–123

### Measurements

Finished case measures 8 x 16cm (3 x 6 ¾ in)

### Materials

- 30cm (12in) square of beige fabric
- 18cm (7in) square of lining fabric
- 4mm Offray Embroidery Ribbon: 1 card each of Dark Moss 571, 846 Blended Bronze and 645 Daffodil
- Anchor Stranded Cotton: 1 skein of Moss Green 269 Matching sewing thread
- One press fastener

### Working embroidery

Using lines of tacking stitches, mark a 16cm (6 ¼ in) square centrally onto fabric. Mark vertical line midway across square to divide it into two equal-sized rectangles. Following Dandelions trace-off pattern on page 110, embroider the four left hand flowers and their stems and leaves only centrally onto one of the two outlined rectangles, using stitches as given on page 74 and colours/ribbons as follows:

### 4mm Offray Embroidery Ribbon

| | |
|---|---|
| Leaves | 571 |
| Flower centres | 846 |
| Flower petals | 645 |

### Anchor Stranded Cotton

| | |
|---|---|
| Stems | 269 |

### Making up

Trim embroidered fabric back to within 1cm (⅜ in) of marked square outline. With right sides facing, fold in half along marked dividing line and stitch along long edge to form a tube, taking 1cm (⅜ in) seam. Remove all tacking lines and press seam open. Make up a lining in exactly the same way. Turn lining right side out and leave embroidered section so that right side is inside. Slip lining inside embroidered section and stitch together around upper edge, taking 1cm ($^3/_8$ in) seam. Press seam open and 1cm ($^3/_8$ in) to wrong side around remaining raw edge of embroidered section. Turn embroidered section right side out and tuck lining inside so that seam between these two falls along upper opening edge. Lay 'tube' flat so that long side seam falls along one fold. Stitch across lower edge of lining section, keeping embroidered section free, to close base of lining. Hand stitch pressed edges of embroidered section together to close base of case, tucking lining seam inside. Attach press fastener to lining inside upper edge to close this opening.

## *Colour Conversion Chart*

This chart gives details of the exact matching shade of Anchor Stranded Cotton for each colour within the Offray Embroidery Ribbon range.

| Offray Embroidery Ribbon | Anchor Stranded Cotton | Offray Embroidery Ribbon | Anchor Stranded Cotton | Offray Embroidery Ribbon | Anchor Stranded Cotton |
|---|---|---|---|---|---|
| 028 | 2 | 570 | 267 | 323 | 186 |
| 463 | 110 | 183 | 88 | 660 | 306 |
| 030 | 403 | 571 | 269 | 327 | 433 |
| 467 | 972 | 203 | 968 | 707 | 328 |
| 095 | 25 | 580 | 210 | 332 | 175 |
| 513 | 214 | 215 | 1021 | 745 | 314 |
| 117 | 24 | 581 | 226 | 344 | 168 |
| 530 | 876 | 235 | 46 | 753 | 324 |
| 140 | 76 | 583 | 188 | 345 | 1039 |
| 550 | 240 | 244 | 42 | 775 | 869 |
| 159 | 74 | 584 | 209 | 430 | 90 |
| 556 | 238 | 260 | 20 | 780 | 72 |
| 161 | 1017 | 587 | 861 | 434 | 870 |
| 563 | 681 | 303 | 1033 | 810 | 275 |
| 168 | 970 | 617 | 292 | 435 | 872 |
| 564 | 877 | 314 | 185 | 824 | 300 |
| 169 | 1028 | 640 | 289 | 447 | 109 |
| 567 | 266 | 315 | 160 | 846 | 355 |
| 178 | 87 | 645 | 301 | | |